The Secret History of the Court of Justinian by Procopius

LITERALLY AND COMPLETELY TRANSLATED FROM THE GREEK FOR THE FIRST TIME

Procopius of Caesarea was born in approximately 500. He is generally considered to be the last major historian of the ancient world. His works have given us a unique and intimate account both of the Roman Military and its Emperor Justinian.

A native of Caesarea in Palaestina Prima little else is known of his early life, and apart from assuming that he would have received a classical Greek Education the rest is deduction rather than based on known facts.

In 527, the first year of Eastern Roman Emperor Justinian I's reign, he became the adsessor (legal adviser) for Belisarius, Justinian's chief military commander who was then starting out on what would become a brilliant military career, initially in the East of the Empire. After early successes Belisarius was defeated in 531 at the Battle of Callinicum and recalled to the Empire's heart in Constantinople.

Justinian was without doubt clever but cruel. When part of Constantinople rose against him in the Nika riots of January, 532, he sent Belisarius and his fellow general Mundo to repress them in a savage massacre in the Hippodrome – witnessed by Procopius.

The following year Procopius accompanied Belisarius on his victorious expedition against the Vandal kingdom in North Africa and took part in the capture of Carthage. Procopius remained in Northern Africa with Belisarius' successor, Solomon the Eunuch, when Belisarius returned to Constantinople.

Procopius rejoined Belisarius for his campaign against the Ostrogothic kingdom in Italy and was there for the Gothic siege of Rome that lasted a year and nine days and ended in March, 538. He witnessed Belisarius' entry into the Gothic capital, Ravenna, in 540.

However at some point in the next few years Procopius seems to have been moved away from working with Belisarius. When the latter was sent back to Italy in 544 to cope with a further outbreak of the war with the Goths, Procopius appears to have no longer been with Belisarius' staff.

Procopius continued to record history and his works are both insightful and clear headed, distilling the complexities of the times into several classic books.

His death is thought to have been around 560.

Index of Contents

PREFACE

INTRODUCTION
Arrangement of the work - The manner in which it has been drawn up - The causes of events omitted in previous writings - The duty of the historian towards posterity - Lessons necessary to tyrants - Semiramis, Sardanapalus, and Nero - Facts relating to Belisarius, Justinian, and Theodora.

CHAPTER I
Birth and character of Antonina - Her marriage with Belisarius - Her adulterous amours - Services rendered by her to the Empress Theodora - Her passion for the Thracian Theodosius - Adoption of the latter - The lovers surprised by Belisarius - His weakness - Revelation made by the slave Macedonia - Flight of Theodosius - Vengeance of Antonina upon Macedonia, and upon Constantine, who had spoken insultingly of her - Theodosius refuses to return to her until the departure of her son Photius - Retirement of Photius - Demands of Theodosius - His return - Infatuation of Belisarius - His return to Byzantium - Theodosius enters a cloister at Ephesus - Despair of Antonina - She causes him to be recalled - His resistance - His secret return.

CHAPTER II
Departure of Belisarius, accompanied by the "consular" Photius, for the war against Chosroes, King of Persia - Antonina remains at Byzantium - Her intrigues against Photius - The latter denounces her adulterous intimacy with Theodosius - Indignation of Belisarius - His agreement with Photius - His vengeance postponed - Entry of the Roman army into Persia - Downfall of John the Cappadocian - Antonina's perjuries - She sets out for the army - Theodosius sent back to Ephesus - Capture of Sisauranum - Arrival of Antonina - Retirement of Belisarius - Arethas and the Saracens - Colchis or Lazica invaded by Chosroes - Capture of Petra - Reverse sustained by Chosroes - The Huns defeated by Valerian - Insurrectionist movement amongst the Persians - Letter of Theodora to Zaberganes - Return of Chosroes to Persia.

CHAPTER III
Arrest of Antonina - Hesitation of Belisarius - Photius repairs to Ephesus, and extorts from Calligonus a confession of his mistress's secrets - Theodosius, having taken refuge in a temple, is given up by Andreas the Bishop - Intervention of Theodora - Photius removes Theodosius, and puts him away in Cilicia - The latter and Calligonus set free - The Empress hands over Antonina's enemies to her - Her vengeance - Punishment of the senator Theodosius - Forced reconciliation between Belisarius and his wife - Arrest of Photius: his firmness under torture - Calligonus restored to Antonina - Theodosius restored to her arms - The Empress's favours - She promises him a high military command - His death from dysentery - Long imprisonment of Photius - Sacred asylums violated - Weakness displayed by the priests - Deliverance of Photius, who enters a convent at Jerusalem - Perjury of Belisarius - His punishment - Failure of the third expedition against Chosroes - Capture of Callinikus - Roman prisoners - Belisarius accused of treachery and cowardice.

CHAPTER IV
Illness of Justinian - Resolutions of the army consequent upon his supposed death - Peter and John the Glutton denounce Belisarius and Buzes - The latter put away and tortured - Disgrace of Belisarius - He is superseded by Martin in the command of the army of the East - His treasures carried away by Theodora - His friendship for Antonina - His letter to Belisarius - Submission of the latter to his wife - Division of his fortune - Betrothal of Joannina, his daughter, to Anastasius, grandson of Theodora - Belisarius appointed Count of the Royal Stable and again commander of the army in Italy - Comparison of the two expeditions.

CHAPTER V
Conduct of Belisarius in Italy - His greed - Defection of Herodianus - Loss of Spoletum - Success of Totila and his Goths - Rupture with John - Betrothal of the latter to Justina, daughter of Germanus - Recall of Belisarius - Perusia taken by the Goths - The marriage between Joannina and Anastasius consummated by a trick on the part of the dying Empress - Return of Antonina, who separates the young pair - Belisarius despised for his weakness - Sergius causes the loss of the Roman army in Africa - Murder of Pegasius by Solomon - The vengeance of Heaven.

CHAPTER VI
History of Justin and his two brothers, poor Illyrian husbandmen - Their enrolment in the army - Their admission into the Palace Guards, in the reign of Leo - Justin condemned to death, during the reign of Anastasius, by the General John Kyrtus, for some breach of discipline - His escape by divine intervention - He becomes praefect of the Praetorian guards - In spite of his ignorance, he is proclaimed Emperor - The way in which he was assisted to sign imperial documents - The Empress Lupicina-Euphemia - Justinian, the nephew of Justin, the real master of the Empire - His cruelty, his avarice, his inconsistency in regard to the laws - He oppresses Italy, Africa, and the rest of the Empire - Amantius condemned, to avenge an outrage upon the bishop John - Perjury towards Vitalianus.

CHAPTER VII
Byzantium divided between two factions: the Blues and the Greens - Justinian puts himself at the head of the former - The Empire entirely upset by the quarrels between these factions - The Blues dress their hair after the manner of the Huns - Their general attire - Their excesses - Behaviour of the Greens - Corruption of the morals of young men - Murder committed with impunity - Inaction on the part of the authorities - Acts of violence committed upon both sexes - A woman throws herself into the sea to save her virtue - Culpability of Justinian - His partiality for the oppressors, upon whom he bestows favours and dignities.

CHAPTER VIII
Calamities in the provinces - Justinian's apathy - Waste of the public money during his reign - Useless presents of money made to the Huns - Extravagance in buildings on the sea-shore - Attack upon the fortunes of private individuals - Description of Justinian's personal appearance - His resemblance to Domitian - Domitian's wife - Alterations in established institutions.

CHAPTER IX
The bear-keeper Acacius, Theodora's father - His widow loses her place in the amphitheatre of the Greens and takes another in that of the Blues - Her daughters - The beginning of Theodora's career - Her precocious immorality - Her accomplishments - Her debaucheries - Her intercourse with Hecebolus, governor of Pentapolis - Her return from the East - Justinian, enamoured of her, wishes to marry her - Assassination of Hypatius - The Praefect Theodotus Colocynthius - Punishment of malefactors - His exile and death.

CHAPTER X
The Empress Euphemia - Her opposition to the marriage of Justinian and Theodora - Justin repeals the law prohibiting the marriage of a patrician with a stage-performer - Justinian and Theodora colleagues on the throne - Death of Justin - Effect of the marriage - Adulation of the senate, clergy, people, and army - General feeling of discouragement - Personal advantages of Theodora - Pretended antagonism between her and Justinian - Theodora deceives the Christians and the factions - Consolidation of despotism.

CHAPTER XI
Legislative innovations - Avarice and cruelty of Justinian - Barbarian invasions provoked - Exorbitant subsidies to the chiefs of the Huns and Chosroes King of Persia, followed by disturbances and violation of truce - Saracens, Slavs, Antes, and other barbarous peoples - Desolation of the provinces - Religious persecutions and confiscation of Church property - Montanists, Sabbatians, Arians, and Samaritans - Pretended conversions - Manicheans and Polytheists - Caesarea, the author's birthplace - Revolt of the peasants under Julian - Hellenism - Law against paederasty - Persecution of astrologers - Continuous emigration.

CHAPTER XII
Downfall and death of Zeno, grandson of Anthemius, Emperor of the West - Robbery of Tatian, Demosthenes, the wealthy Hilara, Dionysus of Libanus and John of Edessa - Forged wills - Theodora and Justinian evil spirits, not simple human beings - Justinian the putative son of Sabbatius - His mother's intimate relations with a spirit - The adventure of a monk - Justinian's temperate manner of living - His fondness for women - Theodora's intercourse with a spirit - Reputation of Macedonia during Justin's time - Her prediction to Theodora - Dream of her marriage with the Prince of the Demons.

CHAPTER XIII
Justinian's qualities - His accessibility - His partiality for the clergy - His gifts to the churches - His passion for blood and money, shared by him with Theodora - Flattery of Tribonianus - Justinian's fickleness and ill-faith - Venality of justice - Corruption of officials - Justinian's fasting and temperate mode of life.

CHAPTER XIV
Abolition of various old customs - The attributes of the quaestor and imperial secretaries - The senate a mere cipher - Corruption of the "Referendaries" - Guilty conduct of Zeno, the Cilician.

CHAPTER XV
Cruelty of Theodora - Her voluptuous life - Her ambition - Her character and Justinian's compared - Her harshness towards persons of rank - Their servility - Pretended mildness of Justinian - Theodora's eagerness for vengeance - Her partiality - The insult offered by her to a patrician - Her stay at Heraeum, on the sea-shore.

CHAPTER XVI
Assassination of Amalasunta, Queen of the Goths, by Peter, Theodora's agent - The secretary, Priscus, obliged to enter a cloister - Justinian's hypocrisy - Disgrace of Areobindus, Theodora's lover - Her way of getting rid of persons of rank - Punishment of Basianus - False accusation against Diogenes, a member of the municipal council - Suborning of witnesses - Theodora's courage.

CHAPTER XVII
Murder of Callinicus, governor of Cilicia - His property confiscated by Justinian - Theodora's severe measures against prostitutes - She compels two girls of noble birth to marry - Her frequent abortions - Disappearance of her natural son, John - Corrupt morals of the ladies of the capital - Theodora disposes of ecclesiastical dignities - Takes upon herself the general superintendence of marriages - Adventure of Saturninus - Persecution of John of Cappadocia.

CHAPTER XVIII
Justinian, a devil in the form of a man, causes the destruction of millions of men - His policy towards the Vandals, Goths, and other barbarians - Chosroes and the Persians - Invasion of the Huns, Saracens, and others - Justinian's theological studies - Religious persecution - Divine anger - Inundations, earthquakes, and the plague.

CHAPTER XIX
A dream relating to Justinian's avarice - The vast treasures of Anastasius squandered by Justinian - He makes himself master of the fortunes of private individuals by false accusations, and squanders them in presents of money to the barbarians, who plunder the Empire - Fulfilment of the dream.

CHAPTER XX

Justinian impoverishes private individuals by "monopolies" - Two new magistrates appointed at Constantinople - Praetor of the People to judge cases of robbery - Legislation in regard to paederasty and female morality - Establishment of an inquisition against heretics - Condemnations and confiscations - Degradation of the quaestorship in the hands of Junilus and Constantine - Their venality.

CHAPTER XXI
The impost called "Aerikon" - Exactions authorised by Justinian - The property of John the Cappadocian confiscated - The farming of the taxes entrusted to salaried commissioners - Increased spoliation - Oath taken against venality - Increasing corruption of officials - The Thracians and Illyrians at first check the depredations of the Huns, Goths, and other barbarians, and then, in turn, take to plundering themselves.

CHAPTER XXII
John of Cappadocia replaced by Theodotus, and Theodotus by Peter Barsyames, the Syrian, an old usurer - His greed - He suppresses the gratuities to the soldiers - Traffic in every kind of employment - Speculation in wheat - Scarcity of provisions at Byzantium - Discontent - Barsyames upheld by Theodora and his own sorceries - His connection with the Manicheans - Their influence over Justinian - Barsyames supersedes John of Palestine as treasury minister - He abolishes the assistance rendered to the unfortunate.

CHAPTER XXIII
Ruin of private properties - Abolition of the remission of arrears of taxes, even in the case of cities taken by the barbarians - The imposts called Syn[=o]n[=e], Epibol[=e], and Diagraph[=e] - Soldiers billeted in private houses.

CHAPTER XXIV
Oppression of the soldiers by the Logothetes - Division of the soldiers into three classes - Their promotion suspended - Their pay diverted to other purposes - The diminishing army - Praetorian soldiers disbanded - Alexander the Logothete in Italy - The general's aides-de-camp - The frontier garrisons abandoned - Palace guards, Scholares, and supernumeraries - Armenians - Peter, the Master of Offices, the murderer of Amalasunta - Palace officials, Domestics, and Protectors - Suppression of the quinquennial gratuity - The imperial officers and dignitaries.

CHAPTER XXV
Unjust treatment of merchants, mariners, and artisans - The straits of the Bosphorus and the Hellespont burdened with custom-house dues - Enormous dues levied by Addeus in the port of Byzantium - Change in the silver coinage: its depreciation - Monopoly of the silk trade - Ruin of Berytus and Tyre - Malversations of Peter Barsyames and his successors - Tyranny of Theodora and avarice of Justinian.

CHAPTER XXVI
Destruction of city decorations and ornaments - Advocates deprived of their fees by the institution of arbitrators - Physicians and professors deprived of their pensions - Public spectacles discontinued - The consulship suppressed - Scarcity of corn and water at Byzantium, Rome, and Alexandria - Generosity of Theodoric, the conqueror of Italy - Greed of Alexander Forficula - Disbanding of the garrison of Thermopylae - Spoliation of Athens and other Greek cities - Hephaestus and Diocletian.

CHAPTER XXVII
Conduct of Justinian and Theodora in regard to the clergy and council of Chalcedon - Arsenius the Samaritan persecutes the Christians of Scythopolis with impunity - Paul, archbishop of Alexandria,

has the deacon Psoes put to death - Rhodon, the governor, by his orders, tortures him: but he is dismissed, and then put to death, together with Arsenius, through the influence of Theodora - Liberius, the new governor, and Pelagius, legate of Pope Vigilius at Alexandria, depose Paul, who buys back the favour of Justinian - Resistance of Vigilius - Faustinus, governor of Palestine, denounced by the Christians as a Samaritan - His condemnation by the Senate - The sentence annulled by Justinian - Outrages upon the Christians.

CHAPTER XXVIII
Laws changed for money considerations - Affair of the church of Emesa - Priscus the forger - A hundred years' prescription granted to the churches - Mission of Longinus - Persecution of the Jews at the Passover - Justinian's intolerance.

CHAPTER XXIX
Justinian's hypocrisy - Letters sent to both Liberius and John Laxarion, confirming them as governors of Egypt - Intervention of Pelagius and Eudaemon - Murder of John - Liberius acquitted by the Senate - Fine inflicted by Justinian - Confiscation of the inheritances of Eudaemon, Euphratas, and Irenaeus - New law as to the inheritances of municipal councillors - Spoliation of the daughter of Anatolia and Ascalon, the widow of Mamilianus - Affair of Tarsus - Malthanes and the Blues of Cilicia - Unpunished assassinations - Justinian's corruptness - Leo the Referendary.

CHAPTER XXX
The "posts" and "spies" - Rapidity of the imperial couriers - Their chief routes - Superiority of the Persians - Reverses of the Romans in Lazica at the hands of Chosroes - The army commissariat - Spoliation of the lawyer Evangelius - Justinian's sarcasm - He and Theodora required their feet to be kissed by those who had audience of them - Their titles of "master" and "mistress" - The palace crowded by applicants for audiences - The death of Justinian alone will show how the vast wealth of the Empire has been spent.

PREFACE

Procopius, the most important of the Byzantine historians, was born at Caesarea in Palestine towards the beginning of the sixth century of the Christian era. After having for some time practised as a "Rhetorician," that is, advocate or jurist, in his native land, he seems to have migrated early to Byzantium or Constantinople. There he gave lessons in elocution, and acted as counsel in several law-cases. His talents soon attracted attention, and he was promoted to official duties in the service of the State. He was commissioned to accompany the famous Belisarius during his command of the army in the East, in the capacity of Counsellor or Assessor: it is not easy to define exactly the meaning of the Greek term, and the functions it embraced. The term "Judge-Advocate" has been suggested[1], a legal adviser who had a measure of judicial as well as administrative power. From his vivid description of the early years of Justinian's reign, we may conclude that he spent some considerable time at the Byzantine court before setting out for the East, at any rate, until the year 532, when Belisarius returned to the capital: he would thus have been an eye-witness of the "Nika" sedition, which, had it not been for the courage and firmness displayed by Theodora, would probably have resulted in the flight of Justinian, and a change of dynasty.

In 533 he accompanied Belisarius on his expedition to Africa. On the way, he was intrusted with an important mission to Sicily. He appears to have returned to Byzantium with Belisarius in 535. He is heard of again, in 536, as charged with another mission in the neighbourhood of Rome, which shows that, at the end of 535, he had accompanied Belisarius, who had been despatched to Italy and Sicily to conquer the territory in the occupation of the Goths. This expedition terminated successfully by the surrender of Vitiges and his captivity at Byzantium in 540.

As the reward of his services, Justinian bestowed upon him the title of "Illustrious" (Illustris), given to the highest class of public officials, raised him to the rank of a Senator, and, finally, appointed him Praefect of Byzantium in 562. He does not, however, seem to have been altogether satisfied: he complains of having been ill-paid for his labours; for several years he was even without employment. This is all that is known of his life. He died shortly before or after the end of the reign of Justinian (565), when he would have been over sixty years of age.

His career seems to have been as satisfactory as could be reasonably expected, all things being taken into consideration; but the violent hatred displayed by him against Justinian in the "Anecdota" or "Secret History", if the work be really his[2] appears to show that he must have had some real or imaginary grounds of complaint; but history throws no light upon these incidents of his political career.

Another question which has been much discussed by the commentators is: "What were the religious opinions of Procopius?"

His own writings do not decide the question; he seems to shew a leaning towards heathenism and Christianity alternately. The truth seems to be that, being of a sceptical turn of mind, he was indifferent; but that, living under an orthodox Emperor, he affected the forms and language of Christianity. Had he been an open and avowed adherent of Paganism, he would scarcely have been admitted to the Senate or appointed to the important official position of Praefect of Byzantium. His description of the plague of 543, which is exceedingly minute in its details, has given rise to the idea that he was a physician, but there is no proof of this. The same thing might have been with equal justice said of Thucydides; or we might assert that Procopius was an architect, on the strength of his having written the "Buildings."

Procopius, holding a position in a period of transition between classical Greek and Byzantine literature, is the first and most talented of Byzantine historians. His writings are characterized by an energetic combination of the Attic models of the affected, but often picturesque style employed by the Byzantine writers. Although he is not free from errors of taste, he expresses his ideas with great vigour, and his thoughts are often worthy of a better age. The information which he has given us is exceedingly valuable. He had ample opportunities of observation, and his works present us with the best picture of the reign of Justinian, so important in Greco-Roman annals.

His chief work is the "Histories," in eight books: two on the Persian wars (408-553), two on the Vandal wars (395-545), and four[3] on the Gothic wars, bringing down the narrative to the beginning of 559. The whole work is very interesting; the descriptions are excellent: in the matter of ethnographical details, Procopius may be said to be without a rival among ancient historians.

He shews equal descriptive talent in his work on the "Buildings" of Justinian, a curious and useful work, but spoiled by excessive adulation of the Emperor. Gibbon is of opinion that it was written with the object of conciliating Justinian, who had been dissatisfied with the too independent judgment of the "Histories." If this be the case, we can understand why the historian avenged himself in the "Secret History," which is a veritable chronique scandaleuse of the Byzantine Court from 549-562. Justinian and Theodora, Belisarius and his wife Antonina, are painted in the blackest colours. Belisarius, who is treated with the least severity, is nevertheless represented as weak and avaricious, capable of any meanness in order to retain the favour of the Court and his military commands, which afforded him the opportunity of amassing enormous wealth. As for Antonina and

Theodora, the revelations of the "Secret History" exhibit a mixture of crime and debauchery not less hideous than that displayed by Messalina. Justinian is represented as a monstrous tyrant, at once cunning and stupid, "like an ass," in the words of the historian, and as the wickedest man that ever lived. The author declares that he and his wife are spirits or demons, who have assumed the form of human beings in order to inflict the greatest possible evils upon mankind. These accusations seem to be founded sometimes upon fact, sometimes upon vague rumours and blind gossip. Generally speaking, the author of the "Secret History" seems sincere, but at the same time he shows a narrowness by confounding all Justinian's acts in one sweeping censure, and in attributing to him the most incredible refinements of political perversity. Critics have asked the question whether the author of such a work can be Procopius of Caesarea, the impartial historian of the wars. Direct proofs of authenticity are wanting, since the most ancient authors who attribute it to him, Suidas and Nicephorus Callistus, lived centuries later.[4] But it is easy to understand that a work of this kind could not be acknowledged by its author, or published during the lifetime of Justinian. In later times, it circulated privately, until the lapse of time had rendered the Byzantine Court indifferent to the hideous picture of the vices of a previous age. The work is evidently that of a contemporary of Justinian; it can only have been written by a functionary familiar with the ins and outs of Court intrigue, who had private grievances of his own to avenge. It is true that it sheds little lustre upon the character of Procopius, since it exhibits him as defaming the character of the masters whom he had formerly served and flattered. But this kind of inconsistency is not uncommon in writers of memoirs, who often revenge themselves posthumously by blackening the reputation of their former masters. Although the author writes under the influence of the most violent resentment, there seems no reason to doubt that, although details may be exaggerated, the work on the whole gives a faithful picture of the Byzantine Court of the period.

The following sketch of the "Character and Histories of Procopius" from Gibbon,[5] although modern authorities have taken exception to it in certain points, will be read with interest: "The events of Justinian's reign, which excite our curious attention by their number, variety, and importance, are diligently related by the secretary of Belisarius, a rhetorician, whom eloquence had promoted to the rank of senator and praefect of Constantinople. According to the vicissitudes of courage or servitude, of favour or disgrace, Procopius successively composed the history, the panegyric, and the satire of his own times. The eight books of the Persian, Vandalic, and Gothic wars, which are continued in the five books of Agathias, deserve our esteem as a laborious and successful imitation of the Attic, or at least of the Asiatic, writers of ancient Greece. His facts are collected from the personal experience and free conversations of a soldier, a statesman, and a traveller; his style continually aspires, and often attains, to the merit of strength and elegance; his reflections, more especially in the speeches which he too frequently inserts, contain a rich fund of political knowledge; and the historian, excited by the generous ambition of pleasing and instructing posterity, appears to disdain the prejudices of the people and the flattery of courts. The writings of Procopius were read and applauded by his contemporaries; but, although he respectfully laid them at the foot of the throne, the pride of Justinian must have been wounded by the praise of an hero who perpetually eclipses the glory of his inactive sovereign. The conscious dignity of independence was subdued by the hopes and fears of a slave, and the secretary of Belisarius laboured for pardon and reward in the six books of imperial edifices.[6] He had dexterously chosen a subject of apparent splendour, in which he could loudly celebrate the genius, the magnificence, and the piety of a prince, who, both as a conqueror and legislator, had surpassed the puerile virtues of Cyrus and Themistocles. Disappointment might urge the flatterer to secret revenge, and the first glance of favour might again tempt him to suspend and suppress a libel, in which the Roman Cyrus is degraded into an odious and contemptible tyrant, in which both the Emperor and his consort Theodora are seriously represented as two demons, who had assumed a human form for the destruction of mankind. Such base inconsistency must doubtless sully the reputation and detract from the credit of Procopius; yet, after the venom of his malignity has been suffered to exhale, the residue of the 'Anecdotes,' even the most disgraceful facts, some of which had been tenderly hinted in his public history, are established by their internal evidence, or the authentic monuments of the times."[7] It remains to add that in some passages, owing to imperfections in the text or the involved nature of the sentences, it is difficult to feel sure as to the meaning. In these the translator can only hope to have given a rendering which harmonises with the context and is generally intelligible, even if the Greek does not seem to have been strictly followed.

For a clear and succinct account of the reign of Justinian, the four chapters in Gibbon (xl.-xliv.), which are generally admitted to be the most successful in his great work, should be read.

INTRODUCTION

I have thus described the fortunes of the Romans in their wars up to the present day, as far as possible assigning the description of events to their proper times and places. What follows will not be arranged with the same exactness, but everything shall be written down as it took place throughout the whole extent of the Roman empire. My reason for this is, that it would not have been expedient for me to describe these events fully while those who were their authors were still alive; for, had I done so, I could neither have escaped the notice of the multitude of spies, nor, had I been detected, could I have avoided a most horrible death; for I could not even have relied upon my nearest relatives with confidence. Indeed, I have been forced to conceal the real causes of many of the events recounted in my former books. It will now be my duty, in this part of my history, to tell what has hitherto remained untold, and to state the real motives and origin of the actions which I have already recounted. But, when undertaking this new task, how painful and hard will it be, to be obliged to falter and contradict myself as to what I have said about the lives of Justinian and Theodora: and particularly so, when I reflect that what I am about to write will not appear to future generations either credible or probable, especially when a long lapse of years shall have made them old stories; for which reason I fear that I may be looked upon as a romancer, and reckoned among playwrights. However, I shall have the courage not to shrink from this important work, because my story will not lack witnesses; for the men of to-day, who are the best informed witnesses of these facts, will hand on trustworthy testimony of their truth to posterity. Yet, when I was about to undertake this work, another objection often presented itself to my mind, and for a long time held me in suspense.

I doubted whether it would be right to hand down these events to posterity; for the wickedest actions had better remain unknown to future times than come to the ears of tyrants, and be imitated by them. For most rulers are easily led by lack of knowledge into imitating the evil deeds of their predecessors, and find it their easiest plan to walk in the evil ways of their forefathers.

Later, however, I was urged to record these matters, by the reflection that those who hereafter may wish to play the tyrant will clearly see, in the first place, that it is probable that retribution will fall upon them for the evil that they may do, seeing that this was what befell these people; and, secondly, that their actions and habits of life will be published abroad for all time, and therefore they will perhaps be less ready to transgress. Who, among posterity, would have known of the licentious life of Semiramis, or of the madness of Sardanapalus or Nero, if no memorials of them had been left to us by contemporary writers? The description of such things, too, will not be entirely without value to such as hereafter may be so treated by tyrants; for unhappy people are wont to console themselves by the thought that they are not the only persons who have so suffered. For these reasons, I shall first give a description of the evil wrought by Belisarius, and afterwards I shall describe the misdeeds of Justinian and Theodora.

CHAPTER I

The wife of Belisarius, whom I have spoken of in my previous writings, was the daughter and granddaughter of chariot-drivers, men who had practised their art in the circus at Byzantium and at Thessalonica. Her mother was one of the prostitutes of the theatre. She herself at first lived a lewd life, giving herself up to unbridled debauchery; besides this, she devoted herself to the study of the drugs which had long been used in her family, and learned the properties of those which were essential for carrying out her plans. At last she was betrothed and married to Belisarius, although she had already borne many children.

She formed adulterous connections as soon as she was married, but took pains to conceal the fact, by making use of familiar artifices, not out of any respect for her husband (for she never felt any shame at any crime whatever, and hoodwinked him by enchantments), but because she dreaded the vengeance of the Empress; for Theodora was very bitter against her, and had already shown her teeth. But, after she had made Theodora her humble friend by helping her when in the greatest difficulties, first of all by making away with Silverius, as shall be told hereafter, and afterwards by ruining John of Cappadocia, as I have already described, she became less timid, and, scorning all concealment, shrank from no kind of wickedness.

There was a Thracian youth, named Theodosius, in the household of Belisarius, who by descent was of the Eunomian faith. On the eve of his departure for Libya, Belisarius held the youth over the font, received him into his arms after baptism, and thenceforth made him a member of his household, with the consent of his wife, according to the Christian rite of adoption. Antonina therefore received Theodosius as a son consecrated by religion, and in consequence loved him, paid him especial attention, and obtained complete dominion over him. Afterwards, during this voyage, she became madly enamoured of him, and, being beside herself with passion, cast away all fear of everything human or divine, together with all traces of modesty, and enjoyed him at first in secret, afterwards even in the presence of her servants and handmaidens; for she was by this time so mad with lust, that she disregarded everything that stood in the way of her passion.

Once, when they were at Carthage, Belisarius caught her in the act, but permitted himself to be deceived by his wife. He found them both together in an underground chamber, and was furiously enraged at the sight; but she showed no sign of fear or a desire to avoid him, and said, "I came to this place with this youth, to hide the most precious part of our plunder, that the Emperor might not come to know of it." This she said by way of an excuse, and he, pretending to be convinced, let it pass, although he saw that the belt which held Theodosius's drawers over his private parts was undone; for he was so overpowered by his love for the creature that he preferred not to believe his own eyes. However, Antonina's debauchery went on from bad to worse, till it reached a shameful pitch. All who beheld it were silent, except one slave woman, named Macedonia, who, when Belisarius was at Syracuse after the conquest of Sicily, first made her master swear the most solemn oaths that he never would betray her to her mistress, and then told him the whole story, bringing as her witnesses two boys who attended on Antonina's bed-chamber.

When Belisarius heard this, he told some of his guards to make away with Theodosius, but the latter, being warned in time, fled to Ephesus: for the greater part of Belisarius's followers, influenced by the natural weakness of his character, were at more pains to please his wife than to show their devotion to him; and this was why they disclosed to her the orders they had received concerning Theodosius. When Constantine saw Belisarius's sorrow at what had befallen him, he sympathized with him, but was so imprudent as to add: "For my own part, I would have killed the woman rather than the youth."

This having been reported to Antonina, she conceived a secret hatred for him, until she could make him feel the weight of her resentment; for she was like a scorpion, and knew how to hide her venom.

Not long afterwards, either by enchantments or by caresses, she persuaded her husband that the accusation brought against her was false; whereupon, without any hesitation, he sent for Theodosius, and promised to deliver up to his wife Macedonia and the boys, which he afterwards did. It is said that she first cut out their tongues, and then ordered them to be hewn in pieces, put into sacks and thrown into the sea. In this bloody deed she was assisted by one of her slaves named Eugenius, who had also been one of those who perpetrated the outrage on Silverius.

Shortly afterwards, Belisarius was persuaded by his wife to kill Constantine. What I have already recounted about Praesidius and his daggers belongs to this period. Belisarius would have let him go, but Antonina would not rest until she had exacted vengeance for the words which I have just repeated. This murder stirred up a great hatred against Belisarius on the part of the Emperor and of the chief nobles of the Empire.

Such was the course of events. Meanwhile, Theodosius refused to return to Italy, where Belisarius and Antonina were then staying, unless Photius were sent out of the way; for Photius was naturally disposed to show his spite against anyone who supplanted him in another's good graces; but he was quite right in feeling jealous of Theodosius, because he himself, although Antonina's son, was quite neglected, whereas the other was exceedingly powerful and had amassed great riches. They say that he had taken treasure amounting to a hundred centenars of gold [about £400,000] from the treasure-houses of the two cities of Carthage and Ravenna, since he had obtained sole and absolute control of the management of them.

When Antonina heard this determination of Theodosius, she never ceased to lay traps for her son and to concoct unnatural plots against him, until she made him see that he must leave her and retire to Byzantium; for he could no longer endure the designs against his life. At the same time she made Theodosius return to Italy, where she enjoyed to the full the society of her lover, thanks to the easy good-nature of her husband. Later on, she returned to Byzantium in company with both of them. It was there that Theodosius became alarmed lest their intimacy should become known, and was greatly embarrassed, not knowing what to do. That it could remain undetected to the end he felt was impossible, for he saw that the woman was no longer able to conceal her passion, and indulge it in secret, but was an open and avowed adulteress, and did not blush to be called so.

For this reason he returned to Ephesus, and after having submitted to the tonsure, joined the monastic order. At this Antonina entirely lost her reason, showed her distress by putting on mourning and by her general behaviour, and roamed about the house, wailing and lamenting (even in the presence of her husband) the good friend she had lost, so faithful, so pleasant, so tender a companion, so prompt in action. At last she even won over her husband, who began to utter the same lamentations. The poor fool kept calling for the return of his well-beloved Theodosius, and afterwards went to the Emperor and besought him and the Empress, till he prevailed upon them to send for Theodosius, as a man whose services always had been and always would be indispensable in the household. Theodosius, however, refused to obey, declaring that it was his fixed determination to remain in the cloister and embrace the monastic life. But this language was by no means sincere, for it was his intention, as soon as Belisarius left the country, to rejoin Antonina by stealth at Byzantium, as, in fact, he did.

CHAPTER II

Shortly afterwards Belisarius was sent by the Emperor to conduct the war against Chosroes, and Photius accompanied him. Antonina remained behind, contrary to her usual custom; for, before this, she had always desired to accompany her husband on all his travels wherever he went, for fear that, when he was by himself, he might return to his senses, and, despising her enchantments, form a true estimate of her character. But now, in order that Theodosius might have free access to her, Antonina began to intrigue in order to get Photius out of her way. She induced some of Belisarius's suite to lose no opportunity of provoking and insulting him, while she herself wrote letters almost every day, in which she continually slandered her son and set every one against him. Driven to bay, the young man was forced to accuse his mother, and, when a witness arrived from Byzantium who told him of Theodosius's secret commerce with Antonina, Photius led him straightway into the presence of Belisarius and ordered him to reveal the whole story. When Belisarius learned this, he flew into a furious rage, fell at Photius's feet, and besought him to avenge him for the cruel wrongs which he had received at the hands of those who should have been the last to treat him in such a manner. "My dearest boy," he exclaimed, "you have never known your father, whoever he may have been, for he ended his life while you were still in your nurse's arms; his property has been of little or no assistance to you, for he was by no means wealthy. Bred under my care, though I was but your stepfather, you have now reached an age when you are capable of assisting me to avenge the wrongs from which I suffer. I have raised you to the consulship, and have heaped riches upon you, so that I may justly be regarded by you as your father, your mother, and your whole family; for it is not by the ties of blood but by deeds that men are accustomed to measure their attachment to each other. The hour has now come when you must not remain an indifferent spectator of the ruin of my house and of the loss with which I am threatened, of so large a sum of money, nor of the immeasurable shame which your mother has incurred in the sight of all men. Remember that the sins of women reflect disgrace not only on their husbands, but also upon their children, whose honour suffers all the more because of their natural likeness to their mothers.

"Be well assured that, for my own part, I love my wife with all my heart; and should it be granted to me to punish the dishonourer of my house, I will do her no hurt; but, as long as Theodosius remains alive, I cannot condone her misconduct."

On hearing these words Photius replied that he would do all that he could to aid his stepfather, but, at the same time, he feared that he himself might come to some harm by so doing; for he was unable to feel any confidence in Belisarius, because of his weakness of character, especially where his wife was concerned. He dreaded the fate of Macedonia, and of many other victims. For this reason he insisted that Belisarius should swear fidelity to him by the most sacred oaths known to Christians, and they bound themselves never to abandon each other, even at the cost of their lives.

For the present, they both agreed that it would be unwise to make any attempt; and they resolved to wait until Antonina had left Byzantium to join them, and Theodosius had returned to Ephesus, which would give Photius the opportunity of going thither and easily disposing of both Theodosius and his fortune. They had just invaded the Persian territory with all their forces, and during this time the ruin of John of Cappadocia was accomplished at Byzantium, as I have told in the former books of my history. I have there only been silent, through fear, on one point, that it was not by mere hazard that Antonina succeeded in deceiving John and his daughter, but by numerous oaths, sworn on all that Christians deem most holy, she made them believe that she intended to do them no harm.

After this, having risen greatly in favour with the Empress, she sent Theodosius to Ephesus, and herself, foreseeing no trouble, set out for the East.

Belisarius had just captured the fortress of Sisauranum, when he was told of his wife's arrival; whereupon he immediately ordered his army to turn back, disregarding the interests of the Empire for the sake of his private feelings. Certain matters had indeed happened, as I have already set forth, which made a retreat advisable, but his wife's presence hastened it considerably. But, as I said at the beginning, I did not then think it safe to describe the real motives of men's actions.

Belisarius was reproached by all the Romans for having sacrificed the interests of his country to his domestic affairs. The reason was that, in his first transport of passion against his wife, he could not bring himself to go far away from Roman territory; for he felt that the nearer he was, the easier it would be for him to take vengeance upon Theodosius, as soon as he heard of the arrival of Antonina.

He therefore ordered Arethas and his people to cross the river Tigris, and they returned home, without having performed anything worthy of record, while he himself took care not to retire more than an hour's journey from the Roman frontier. The fortress of Sisauranum, indeed, for an active man, is not more than a day's journey from the frontier by way of Nisibis, and only half that distance if one goes by another route. But had he chosen to cross the river Tigris at first with all his host, I have no doubt that he would have been able to carry off all the riches of Assyria, and extend his conquests as far as the city of Ctesiphon, without meeting with any opposition. He might even have secured the release of the Antiochians, and all the other Romans who were there in captivity, before returning home.

Furthermore, he was chiefly to blame for the extreme ease with which Chosroes led his army home from Colchis. I will now relate how this came to pass. When Chosroes, the son of Cabades, invaded Colchis, with the result which I have recounted elsewhere, and took Petra, the Medes nevertheless sustained severe losses, both in battle and owing to the difficulties of the country; for, as I have said already, Lazica is a country almost inaccessible, owing to its rocks and precipices. They had at the same time been attacked by pestilence, which carried off the greater part of the troops, and many died from want of food and necessaries. It was at this crisis of affairs that certain men from Persia came into that country, bringing the news that Belisarius had beaten Nabedes in a battle near the city of Nisibis, and was pressing forward; that he had taken the fortress of Sisauranum, and had made prisoners of Bleschames and eight hundred Persian lancers; that another corps of Romans under Arethas, the chief of the Saracens, had been detached to cross the Tigris, and ravage the land to the east of that river, which up to that time had remained free from invasion.

It happened also that the army of Huns, whom Chosroes had sent into Roman Armenia, in order, by this diversion, to prevent the Romans from hindering his expedition against the Lazi, had fallen in with and been defeated by Valerian, at the head of a Roman army, and almost annihilated. When this news was brought to the Persians, having been reduced to desperate straits by their ill success at Lazica, they feared that, if an army should cut them off in their critical position, they might all die of hunger amidst the crags and precipices of that inaccessible country. They feared, too, for their children, their wives and their country; and all the flower of Chosroes' army railed bitterly at him for having broken his plighted word and violated the common law of nations, by invading a Roman State in a most unwarrantable manner, in time of peace, and for having insulted an ancient and most powerful State which he would not be able to conquer in war. The soldiers were on the point of breaking out into revolt, had not Chosroes, alarmed at the state of affairs, discovered a remedy for it. He read to them a letter which the Empress had just written to Zaberganes, in the following terms:

"You must know, O Zaberganes, since you were ambassador at our Court not long ago, that we are well disposed towards you, and that we do not doubt that you have our interests at heart. You will easily realise the good opinion which I have formed of you, if you will persuade King Chosroes to maintain peaceful relations with our empire. I promise you, in that case, the fullest recompense on the part of my husband, who never does anything without my advice."

When Chosroes had read this, he reproachfully asked the spokesmen of the Persians whether they thought that that was an Empire which was managed by a woman, and thus managed to quell their impetuosity; but, nevertheless, he retired from his position in alarm, expecting that his retreat would be cut off by Belisarius and his forces; but, as he found himself unopposed on his march, he gladly made his way home.

CHAPTER III

When Belisarius entered Roman territory, he found that his wife had arrived from Byzantium. He kept her in custody in disgrace, and was frequently minded to put her to death, but had not the heart to do so, being overpowered, I believe, by the ardour of his love. Others, however, say that his mind and resolution were destroyed by the enchantments which his wife employed against him.

Meanwhile, Photius arrived in a state of fury at Ephesus, having taken with him in chains Calligonus, a eunuch and pander of Antonina, whom, by frequently flogging him during the journey, he forced to tell all his mistress's secrets. Theodosius, however, was warned in time, and took sanctuary in the temple of St. John the Apostle, which is revered in that town as a most sacred spot; but Andrew, the bishop of Ephesus, was bribed into delivering him up into the hands of Photius.

Meanwhile, Theodora was very anxious about Antonina, when she heard what had befallen her. She summoned both Belisarius and his wife to Byzantium: on hearing this, Photius sent Theodosius away to Cilicia, where his own spearmen were in winter quarters, giving orders to his escort to take the man thither as secretly as possible, and, when they arrived at Cilicia, to guard him with exceeding strictness, and not to let anyone know in what part of the world he was. He himself, with Calligonus and Theodosius's treasures, which were very considerable, repaired to Byzantium.

At that juncture, the Empress clearly proved to all that she knew how to recompense the murderous services which Antonina had rendered her, by even greater crimes committed to further her plans. Indeed, Antonina had only betrayed one man to her by her wiles, her enemy John of Cappadocia, but the Empress caused the death of a large number of innocent persons, whom she sacrificed to the vengeance of Antonina. The intimates of Belisarius and Photius were some of them flogged, although the only charge against them was their friendship for these two persons; and no one, to the present day, knows what afterwards became of them; while she sent others into exile, who were accused of the same crime, friendship for Photius and Belisarius. One of those who accompanied Photius to Ephesus, Theodosius by name, although he had attained the rank of senator, was deprived of all his property, and imprisoned by Theodora in an underground dungeon, where she kept him fastened to a kind of manger by a rope round his neck, which was so short that it was always quite tense and never slack. The wretched man was always forced to stand upright at this manger, and there to eat and sleep, and do all his other needs; there was no difference between him and an ass, save that he did not bray. No less than four months were passed by him in this condition, until he was seized with melancholy and became violently mad, upon which he was released from his prison and soon afterwards died.

As for Belisarius, she forced him against his will to become reconciled to his wife Antonina. Photius, by her orders, was tortured like a slave, and was beaten with rods upon the back and shoulders, and ordered to disclose where Theodosius and the pander eunuch were. But he, although cruelly tortured, kept the oath which he had sworn inviolate; and although he was naturally weak and delicate, and had always been forced to take care of his health, and had never had any experience of ill-treatment or discomfort of any kind, yet he never revealed any of Belisarius's secrets.

But afterwards all that had hitherto been kept secret came to light. Theodora discovered the whereabouts of Calligonus, and restored him to Antonina. She also found where Theodosius was, and had him conveyed to Byzantium, and, on his arrival, concealed him straightway in the palace. On the morrow she sent for Antonina, and said to her, "Dearest lady, a pearl fell into my hands yesterday, so beautiful that I think no one has ever seen its like. If you would like to see it, I will not grudge you the sight of it, but will gladly show it to you."

Antonina, who did not understand what was going on, begged eagerly to be shown the pearl, whereupon Theodora led Theodosius by the hand out of the chamber of one of her eunuchs and displayed him to her. Antonina was at first speechless through excess of joy, and when she had recovered herself, warmly protested her gratitude to Theodora, whom she called her saviour, her benefactress, and truly her mistress. Theodora kept Theodosius in her palace, treated him with every luxury, and even boasted that, before long, she would appoint him generalissimo of the Roman armies. But divine justice, which carried him off through dysentery, prevented this.

Theodora had at her disposal secret and absolutely secluded dungeons, so solitary and so dark that it was impossible to distinguish between night and day. In one of these she kept Photius imprisoned for a long time. He managed, however, to escape, not only once, but twice. The first time he took sanctuary in the Church of the Mother of God, which is one of the most sacred and famous churches in Byzantium, wherein he sat as a suppliant at the holy table; but she ordered him to be removed by main force and again imprisoned. The second time he fled to the Church of St. Sophia, and suddenly took refuge in the holy font, which is held in reverence by Christians above all other places; but the woman was able to drag him even from thence, for to her no place ever was sacred or unassailable; and she thought nothing of violating the holiest of sanctuaries. The Christian priests and people were struck with horror at her impiety, but nevertheless yielded and submitted to her in everything.

Photius had lived in this condition for nearly three years, when the prophet Zacharias appeared to him in a dream, commanded him to escape, and promised his assistance. Relying upon this vision, he rose, escaped from his prison, and made his way to Jerusalem in disguise; though tens of thousands must have seen the youth, yet none recognised him. There he shaved off all his hair, assumed the monastic habit, and in this manner escaped the tortures which Theodora would have inflicted upon him.

Belisarius took no account of the oaths which he had sworn, and made no effort to avenge Photius's sufferings, in spite of the solemn vows which he had made to do so. Hereafter, probably by God's will, all his warlike enterprises failed. Some time afterwards he was dispatched against the Medes and Chosroes, who had for the third time invaded the Roman Empire, and fell under suspicion of treachery, although he was considered to have performed a notable achievement in driving the enemy away from the frontier; but when Chosroes, after crossing the Euphrates, took the populous city of Callinikus without a blow, and made slaves of tens of thousands of Romans, Belisarius remained quiet, and never so much as offered to attack the enemy, whereby he incurred the reproach of either treachery or cowardice.

CHAPTER IV

About this time Belisarius underwent another disgrace. The people of Byzantium were ravaged by the pestilence of which I have already spoken. The Emperor Justinian was attacked by it so severely that it was reported that he had died. Rumour spread these tidings abroad till they reached the Roman camp, whereupon some of the chief officers said that, if the Romans set up any other emperor in Byzantium, they would not acknowledge him. Shortly after this, the Emperor recovered from his malady, whereupon the chiefs of the army accused one another of having used this language. The General Peter, and John, surnamed "The Glutton," declared that Belisarius and Buzes had used the words which I have just quoted. The Empress Theodora, thinking that these words applied to herself, was greatly enraged. She straightway summoned all the commanders to Byzantium to make an inquiry into the matter, and suddenly sent for Buzes to come into her private apartments, on the pretext of discussing important matters of business with him. There was in the palace an underground building, which was securely fastened, and as complicated as a labyrinth, and which might be compared to the nether world, wherein she kept imprisoned most of those who had offended her. Into this pit she cast Buzes; and although he was of a consular family, nothing was known for certain concerning him; as he sat in the darkness, he could not tell day from night; nor could he ask, for he who flung him his daily food never spoke, but acted like one dumb beast with another. All thought him dead, but none dared to mention him or allude to him. Two years and four months afterwards, Theodora relented and released him, and he appeared in the world like one raised from the dead; but ever afterwards he was short-sighted and diseased in body. Such was the fate of Buzes.

Belisarius, although none of the charges brought against him could be proved, was removed by the Emperor, at the instance of Theodora, from the command of the army in the East, which was given to Martinus. The command of the Doryphori[8] and Hypaspitæ[9] of Belisarius, and of those of his servants who had distinguished themselves in war, was by his orders divided amongst the generals and certain of the palace eunuchs. They cast lots for these soldiers, together with their arms, and divided them amongst themselves as the lot fell. As for his friends and the many people who had before served under him, Justinian forbade them to visit him. Thus was seen in the city a piteous spectacle which men could scarce believe to be real, that of Belisarius simply a private individual, almost alone, gloomy and thoughtful, ever dreading to be set upon and assassinated.

When the Empress learned that he had amassed much treasure in the East; she sent one of the palace eunuchs to fetch it away to the Court. Antonina, as I have already said, was now at variance with her husband, and the nearest and dearest friend of the Empress, because she had just destroyed John of Cappadocia. To please Antonina, the Empress arranged everything in such a fashion that she appeared to have pleaded for her husband's pardon, and to have saved him from these great disasters; whereby the unhappy man not only became finally reconciled to her, but her absolute slave, as though he had been preserved by her from death. This was brought about as follows:

One day Belisarius came early to the palace as usual, accompanied by a small and miserable retinue. He was ungraciously received by the Emperor and Empress, and even insulted in their presence by low-born villains. He went home towards evening, often turning himself about, and looking in every direction for those whom he expected to set upon him. In this state of dread, he went up to his chamber, and sat down alone upon his couch, without a brave man's spirit, and scarce remembering that he had ever been a man, but bathed with sweat, his head dizzy, trembling and despairing, racked by slavish fears and utterly unmanly thoughts. Antonina, who knew nothing of what was going on, and was far from expecting what was about to come to pass, kept walking up and down the hall, on pretence of suffering from heartburn; for they still regarded each other with suspicion. Meanwhile, an officer of the palace, named Quadratus, came just after sunset, passed through the court, and suddenly appeared at the door of the men's apartments, saying that he brought a message from the Empress.

Belisarius, on hearing him approach, drew up his hands and feet on to the bed, and lay on his back in the readiest posture to receive the final stroke, so completely had he lost his courage.

Quadratus, before entering, showed him the Empress' letter. It ran as follows:

"You are not ignorant, my good sir, of all your offences against me; but I owe so much to your wife, that I have determined to pardon all your offences for her sake, and I make her a present of your life. For the future you may be of good cheer as regards your life and fortune: we shall know by your future conduct what sort of husband you will be to your wife!"

When Belisarius read this, he was greatly excited with joy, and, as he wished at the same time to give some present proof of his gratitude, he straightway rose, and fell on his face at his wife's feet. He embraced her legs with either hand, and kissed the woman's ankles and the soles of her feet, declaring that it was to her that he owed his life and safety, and that hereafter he would be her faithful slave, and no longer her husband.

The Empress divided Belisarius's fortune into two parts; she gave thirty centenars of gold to the Emperor, and allowed Belisarius to keep the rest. Such was the fortune of the General Belisarius, into whose hands Fate had not long before given Gelimer and Vitiges as prisoners of war. The man's wealth had for a long time excited the jealousy of Justinian and Theodora, who considered it too great, and fit only for a king. They declared that he had secretly embezzled most of the property of Gelimer and Vitiges, which belonged to the State, and that he had restored a small part alone, and one hardly worthy of an Emperor's acceptance. But, when they thought of what great things the man had done, and how they would raise unpopular clamour against themselves, especially as they had no ground whatever for accusing him of peculation, they desisted; but, on this occasion, the Empress, having surprised him at a time when he was quite unmanned by fear, managed at one stroke to become mistress of his entire fortune; for she straightway established a relationship between them, betrothing Joannina, Belisarius's only daughter, to her grandson Anastasius.

Belisarius now asked to be restored to his command, and to be nominated general of the army of the East, in order to conduct the war against Chosroes and the Medes, but Antonina would not permit this; she declared that she had been insulted by her husband in those countries, and never wished to see them again.

For this reason Belisarius was appointed Constable,[10] and was sent for a second time into Italy, with the understanding, they say, with the Emperor, that he should not ask for any money to defray the cost of this war, but should pay all its expenses out of his own private purse. Everyone imagined that Belisarius made these arrangements with his wife and with the Emperor in order that he might get away from Byzantium, and, as soon as he was outside the city walls, straightway take up arms and do some brave and manly deed against his wife and his oppressors. But he made light of all that had passed, forgot the oaths which he had sworn to Photius and his other intimates, and followed his wife in a strange ecstasy of passion for her, though she was already sixty years of age.

When he arrived in Italy, things went wrong with him daily, for he had clearly incurred the enmity of heaven. In his former campaign against Theodatus and Vitiges, the tactics which he had adopted as general, though they were not thought to be suitable to the circumstances, yet, as a rule, turned out prosperously: in this second campaign, he gained the credit of having laid his plans better, as was to be expected from his greater experience in the art of war; but, as matters for the most part turned out ill, people began to have a poor opinion of him and his judgment. So true it is that human affairs are guided, not by men's counsel, but by the influence of heaven, which we commonly call fortune, because we see how events happen, but know not the cause which determines them. Therefore, to that which seems to come to pass without reason is given the name of "chance." But this is a subject upon which everyone must form his own opinion.

CHAPTER V

At the end of Belisarius's second expedition to Italy, he was obliged to retire in disgrace; for, as I have told already, he was unable for a space of five years to effect a landing on the continent, because he had no stronghold there, but spent the whole time in hovering off the coast. Totila was very eager to meet him in the open field, but never found an opportunity, for both the Roman general and all the army were afraid to fight. For this reason he recovered nothing of all that had been lost, but even lost Rome as well, and pretty nearly everything else. During this time he became exceedingly avaricious and greedy for ignoble gain. Because he had received no funds from the Emperor, he plundered all the Italian peoples of Ravenna and Sicily, and the rest of Italy without mercy, by way of exacting vengeance for irregularities in their past lives. Thus he fell upon Herodianus, and asked him for money with the most dreadful threats; whereupon he, in his rage, threw off his allegiance to Rome and went over with his troops to Totila and the Goths, and handed over to them the town of Spoletum.

I will now tell how Belisarius fell out with John, the nephew of Vitalianus, a matter which was exceedingly prejudicial to the interests of Rome. The Empress was so violently incensed against Germanus, and showed her dislike of him so plainly, that no one dared to connect himself with him by marriage, although he was the Emperor's nephew, and his children remained unmarried as long as she lived, while his daughter Justina was also without a husband at the age of eighteen. For this reason, when John was sent by Belisarius on a mission to Byzantium, Germanus was forced to enter upon negotiations with him with a view to marriage with his daughter, although such an alliance was far beneath him. When both had settled the matter to their satisfaction, they bound each other by the most solemn oaths, to use their best endeavours to bring about this alliance; for neither of them trusted the other, as John knew that he was seeking an alliance above his station, and Germanus despaired of finding another husband for his daughter. The Empress was beside herself at this, and endeavoured to thwart them in every possible way; but as her threats had no effect upon either, she openly threatened to put John to death. After this, John was ordered to return to Italy, and, fearing Antonina's designs upon him, held no further communication with Belisarius until her departure for Byzantium; for he had good reason to suspect that the Empress had sent instructions to Antonina to have him murdered; and when he considered the character of Antonina and Belisarius's infatuation for his wife, which made him yield to her in everything, he was greatly alarmed.

From this time forth the power of Rome, which had long been unstable, utterly fell to the ground for want of capable support. Such were the fortunes of Belisarius in the Gothic war. After this, despairing of success, he begged the Emperor to allow him to leave Italy with all speed. When he heard that his prayer had been granted, he joyfully retired, bidding a long farewell to the Roman army and the Italians. He left the greater part of Italy in the enemy's power and Perusia in the last agonies of a terrible siege: while he was on his road home, it was taken, and endured all the miseries of a city taken by assault, as I have already related. In addition to his ill-success abroad, he also had to submit to a domestic misfortune, which came about as follows: The Empress Theodora was eager to bring about the marriage of her grandson, Anastasius, with Belisarius's daughter, and wearied her parents with frequent letters on the subject; but they, not being desirous of contracting this alliance, put off the marriage until they could appear in person at Byzantium, and when the Empress sent for them, made the excuse that they could not leave Italy. But she persisted in her determination to make her grandson master of Belisarius's fortune, for she knew that the girl would be his heiress, as he had no other children. She did not, however, trust Antonina's character, and feared lest, after her own death, Antonina might prove unfaithful to her house, although she had found her so helpful in emergencies, and might break the compact. These considerations prompted her to a most abominable act. She made the boy and girl live together without any marriage ceremony, in violation of the laws. It is said that the girl was unwilling to cohabit with him, and that the Empress had her secretly forced to do so, that the marriage might be consummated by the dishonour of the bride, and so the Emperor might not be able to oppose it. After this had taken place, Anastasius and the girl fell passionately in love with each other, and lived together in this manner for eight months.

Immediately after the Empress's death, Antonina came to Byzantium. She found it easy to ignore the outrage which Theodora had committed upon her, and, without considering that, if she united the girl to another, she would be no better than a harlot, she drove away Theodora's grandson with insults, and forcibly separated her daughter from the man whom she loved.

This action caused her to be regarded as one of the most heartless women upon earth, but nevertheless the mother obtained, without any difficulty, Belisarius's approval of her conduct, on his return home. Thus did this man's true character reveal itself. Although he had sworn a solemn oath to Photius and to several of his intimates and broken it, yet all men readily forgave him, because they suspected that the reason of his faithlessness was not the dominion of his wife over him, but his fear of Theodora; but now that Theodora was dead, as I have told you, he thought nothing about Photius or any of his intimates, but entirely submitted to the sway of his wife, and her pander Calligonus. Then at last all men ceased to believe in him, scorned and flouted him, and railed at him for an idiot. Such were the offences of Belisarius, about which I have been obliged to speak freely in this place.

In its proper place, I have said enough about the shortcomings of Sergius, the son of Bacchus, in Libya. I have told how he was the chief cause of the ruin of the Roman power in that country, how he broke the oath which he swore to the Levathae on the Gospels, and how he, without excuse, put to death the eighty ambassadors. I need only add in this place, that these men did not come to Sergius with any treacherous intent, and that Sergius had not the slightest reason for suspecting them, but having invited them to a banquet and taken an oath not to harm them, he cruelly butchered them.

Solomon, the Roman army, and all the Libyans were lost owing to this crime; for, in consequence of what he had done, especially after Solomon's death, no officer or soldier would expose himself to the dangers of war. John, the son of Sisinniolus, was especially averse to taking the field, out of the hatred which he bore to Sergius, until Areobindus arrived in Libya.

Sergius was effeminate and unwarlike, very young both in years and in mind, excessively jealous and insolent to all men, luxurious in his habits, and inflated with pride. However, after he had become the accepted husband of the niece of Antonina, Belisarius's wife, the Empress would not permit him to be punished in any way or removed from his office, although she saw distinctly that the state of affairs in Libya threatened its utter ruin; and she even induced the Emperor to pardon Solomon, Sergius's brother, for the murder of Pegasius. How this came to pass I will now explain.

After Pegasius had ransomed Solomon from captivity among the Levathae, and the barbarians had returned home, Solomon and Pegasius, who had ransomed him, set out, accompanied by a few soldiers, to Carthage. On the way Pegasius reproached Solomon with the wrong he had done, and bade him remember that Heaven had only just rescued him from the enemy. Solomon, enraged at being taunted with his captivity, straightway slew Pegasius, and thus requited him for having ransomed him. But when Solomon reached Byzantium, the Emperor absolved him from the guilt of murder, on the pretext that he had slain a traitor to the Roman Empire, and gave him letters of acquittal. Solomon, having thus escaped all punishment for his crime, departed gladly for the East, to visit his own country and his family; but the vengeance of God fell upon him on the way, and removed him from amongst mankind. This is what happened in regard to Solomon and Pegasius.

CHAPTER VI

I now come to the description of the private life and character of Justinian and Theodora, and of the manner in which they rent the Roman Empire asunder.

At the time when Leo occupied the imperial throne, three young husbandmen, of Illyrian birth, named Zimarchus, Ditybistus, and Justin of Bederiane, in order to escape from their utter poverty at home, determined to enlist in the army. They made their way to Byzantium on foot, with knapsacks of goat's-hair on their shoulders, containing nothing but a few biscuits which they had brought from home. On their arrival they were enrolled in the army, and chosen by the Emperor amongst the palace guards, being all three very handsome young men.

Afterwards, when Anastasius succeeded to the throne, war broke out with the Isaurians who had rebelled against him. He sent a considerable army against them, under the command of John, surnamed "The Hunchback." This John arrested Justin for some offence and imprisoned him, and on the following day would have put him to death, had not a vision which he beheld in his sleep prevented him. He said that, in his dream, a man of great stature, and in every way more than human, bade him release the man whom he had that day cast into prison. When he awoke, he made light of this vision; and, although he saw again the same vision and heard the same words on the following night, not even then would he obey the command. But the vision appeared for the third time, and threatened him terribly if he did not do what he was commanded, and warned him that he would thereafter stand in great need of this man and his family when his wrath should fall upon him. Thus did Justin escape death.

As time went on, this Justin rose to great power. The Emperor Anastasius appointed him commander of the palace guard, and when that prince died, he, by the influence of his position, seized the throne. He was by this time an old man with one foot in the grave, so utterly ignorant of letters, that one may say that he did not know the alphabet, a thing which had never happened before amongst the Romans. It had been customary for the Emperor to sign the decrees which were issued by him with his own hand, whereas he neither made decrees, nor was capable of conducting affairs; but Proclus, who acted as his quaestor and colleague, arranged everything at his own pleasure. However, in order that the Emperor's signature might appear in public documents, his officers invented the following device. They had the shapes of four Latin letters cut in a thin piece of wood, and then, having dipped the pen in the imperial ink used by the Emperors in writing, they put it in the Emperor's hand, and laying the piece of wood on the paper to be signed, they guided the Emperor's hand and pen round the outline of the four letters, making it follow all the convolutions cut in the wood, and then retired with the result as the Emperor's signature. This was how the affairs of the Empire were managed under Justin. His wife was named Lupicina; she was a slave and a barbarian, whom he had bought for his mistress, and at the close of his life she ascended the throne with him. Justin was not strong enough to do his subjects either good or harm; he was utterly simple, a very poor speaker, and a complete boor. Justinian was his sister's son, who, when quite a young man, practically governed the State, and brought more woe upon the Romans than anyone we have ever heard of before. He was ever ready to commit unrighteous murders and rob men of their estates, and thought nothing of making away with tens of thousands of men who had given him no cause for doing so. He had no respect for established institutions, but loved innovations in everything, and was, in short, the greatest destroyer of all the best of his country's institutions. As for the plague, of which I have made mention in the former books of my history, although it ravaged the whole earth, yet as many men escaped it as perished by it, some of them never taking the contagion, and others recovering from it. But no human being in all the Roman Empire could escape from this man, for he was like some second plague sent down from heaven to prey upon the whole human race, which left no man untouched. Some he slew without cause, others he reduced to a struggle with poverty, so that their case was more piteous than that of the dead, and they prayed daily to be relieved from their misery even by the most cruel death, while he robbed others of their lives and their property at the same time.

Not content with ruining the Roman Empire, he carried out the conquest of Italy and Africa, merely that he might treat them in the same way, and destroy the inhabitants, together with those who were already his subjects. He had not been in authority ten days before he put to death Amantius, the chief of the palace eunuchs, with several others. He had no complaint whatever against the man beyond that he had said something offensive about John the archbishop of the city. Owing to this, he became the most dreaded of all men in the world.

Immediately afterwards he sent for the usurper Vitalianus, to whom he had given the most solemn pledges for his safety, and had partaken of the Christian sacrament with him. Shortly afterwards, he conceived some suspicion of him, and made away with him and his companions in the palace, for no reason whatever, thus showing that he scorned to observe even the most solemn oaths.

CHAPTER VII

In the former part of my history I have explained how the people had long been divided into two factions. Justinian associated himself with one of these, the Blues, which had previously favoured him, and was thus enabled to upset everything and throw all into disorder. Thereby the Roman constitution was beaten to its knees. However, all the Blues did not agree to follow his views, but only those who were inclined to revolutionary measures. Yet, as the evil spread, these very men came to be regarded as the most moderate of mankind, for they used their opportunities of doing wrong less than they might have done. Nor did the revolutionists of the Green faction remain idle, but they also, as far as they were able, continually perpetrated all kinds of excesses, although individuals of their number were continually being punished. This only made them bolder, for men, when they are treated harshly, usually become desperate.

At this time Justinian, by openly encouraging and provoking the Blue faction, shook the Roman Empire to its foundation, like an earthquake or a flood, or as though each city had been taken by the enemy. Everything was everywhere thrown into disorder; nothing was left alone. The laws and the whole fabric of the State were altogether upset, and became the very opposite of what they had been. First of all, the revolutionists altered the fashion of wearing the hair, for they cut it short, in a manner quite different to that of the rest of the Romans. They never touched the moustache and beard, but let them grow like the Persians: but they shaved the hair off the front part of their heads as far as the temples, and let it hang down long and in disorder behind, like the Massagetae. Wherefore they called this the Hunnic fashion of wearing the hair.

In the next place they all chose to wear richly-embroidered dresses, far finer than became their several stations in life, but they were able to pay for them out of their illicit gains. The sleeves of their tunics were made as tight as possible at the wrists, but from thence to the shoulder were of an astounding width, and whenever they moved their hands, in applauding in the theatre or the hippodrome, or encouraging the competitors, this part of the tunic was waved aloft, to convey to the ignorant the impression that they were so beautifully made and so strong that they were obliged to wear such robes as these to cover their muscles. They did not perceive that the empty width of their sleeves only made their bodies appear even more stunted than they were. The cloaks, drawers and shoes which they mostly affected were called after the Huns, and made in their fashion.

At first they almost all openly went about armed at night, but by day hid short two-edged swords upon their thighs under their cloaks. They gathered together in gangs as soon as it became dusk, and robbed respectable people in the market-place and in the narrow lanes, knocking men down and taking their cloaks, belts, gold buckles, and anything else that they had in their hands. Some they murdered as well as robbed, that they might not tell others what had befallen them. These acts roused the indignation of all men, even the least disaffected members of the Blue faction; but as they began not to spare even these, the greater part began to wear brazen belts and buckles and much smaller cloaks than became their station, lest their fine clothes should be their death, and, before the sun set, they went home and hid themselves. But the evil spread, and as the authorities in charge of the people did nothing to punish the criminals, these men became very daring; for crime, when encouraged to manifest itself openly, always increases enormously, seeing that even when punished it cannot be entirely suppressed. Indeed, most men are naturally inclined to evil-doing. Such was the behaviour of the Blues.

As for the opposite faction, some of them joined the bands of their opponents, hoping thus to be able to avenge themselves upon the party which had ill-used them; some fled secretly to other lands, while many were caught on the spot and killed by their adversaries, or by order of the government. A number of young men also joined this party without having previously taken any interest in such matters, being attracted by the power and the licence which it gave them to do evil. Indeed, there was no sort of villany known amongst men which was not committed at this time unpunished.

In the beginning men put away their own opponents, but, as time went on, they murdered men who had done them no hurt. Many bribed the Blues to kill their personal enemies, whom they straightway slew, and declared that they were Greens, though they might never have seen them before. And these things were not done in the dark or by stealth, but at all hours of the day and in every part of the city, before the eyes, as it might be, of the chief men of the State; for they no longer needed to conceal their crimes, because they had no fear of punishment; but to kill an unarmed passer-by with one blow was a sort of claim to public esteem, and a means of proving one's strength and courage.

Life became so uncertain that people lost all expectation of security, for everyone continually had death before his eyes, and no place or time seemed to offer any hope of safety, seeing that men were slain indiscriminately in the holiest churches, and even during divine service. No one could trust friends or relations, for many were slain at the instance of their nearest of kin. No inquiry took place into such occurrences, but these blows fell unexpectedly upon everyone, and no one helped the fallen. Laws and contracts, which were considered confirmed, had no longer any force; everything was thrown into confusion and settled by violence. The government resembled a despotism, not a securely established one, but one which was changed almost daily, and was ever beginning afresh. The minds of the chief magistrates seemed stricken with consternation, and their spirits cowed by fear of one single man. The judges gave sentence on disputed points not according to what they thought to be lawful and right, but according as each of the litigants was a friend or an enemy of the ruling faction; for any judge who disregarded their instructions was punished with death. Many creditors also were compelled by main force to restore their bills to their debtors without having received anything of what was owing them, and many, against their will, had to bestow freedom upon their slaves.

It is said that some ladies were forced to submit to the embraces of their own slaves; and the sons of leading men who had been mixed up with these youths, forced their fathers to hand over their property to them, and to do many other things against their will. Many boys, with their fathers' knowledge, were forced to undergo dishonour at the hands of the Blues, and women living with their own husbands were forced to submit to the like treatment.

We are told that a woman, who was not over-well dressed, was sailing with her husband in a boat towards the suburb across the strait; they met on their way some men of this faction, who took her away from her husband with threats, and placed her in their own boat. When she entered the boat together with these young men, she secretly told her husband to take courage, and not to fear any evil for her. "Never," said she, "will I permit myself to be outraged;" and while her husband was gazing on her with the greatest sorrow, she sprang into the sea, and was never seen again. Such were the outrages which the people of this faction dared to commit in Byzantium.

Yet all this did not so much gall the victims as Justinian's offences against the State; for those who suffer most cruelly from evil-doers are in great part consoled by the expectation that the law and the authorities will avenge them. If they have any hope for the future, men bear their present sufferings with a much lighter heart; but when they are outraged by the established government, they are naturally much more hurt by the evil which befalls them, and the improbability of redress drives them to despair. Justinian's fault was, not only that he turned a deaf ear to the complaints of the injured, but did not even disdain to behave himself as the avowed chief of this party; that he gave great sums of money to these youths, and kept many of them in his own retinue; that he even went so far as to appoint some of them to governments and other official posts.

CHAPTER VIII

These excesses took place not only in Byzantium, but in every city of the Empire: for these disorders were like bodily diseases, and spread from thence over the whole Roman Empire. But the Emperor cared not at all for what was going on, although he daily beheld what took place in the hippodrome, for he was exceedingly stupid, very much like a dull-witted ass, which follows whoever holds its bridle, shaking its ears the while. This behaviour on the part of Justinian ruined everything.

As soon as he found himself the head of his uncle's empire, he at once did his utmost to squander the public treasure over which he now had control. For he lavished wealth extravagantly upon the Huns who from time to time came across and, ever afterwards, the Roman provinces were subjected to constant incursions; for these barbarians, having once tasted our wealth, could not tear themselves away from the road which led to it. Justinian also threw away great sums upon the construction of large moles, as if he thought to restrain the force of the never-resting waves. He ran out stone breakwaters from the beach far into the water to divert the currents of the ocean, and, as it were, to match his wealth against the power of the sea.

As for the private fortunes of individual Romans, he confiscated them for his own use in all parts of the empire, either by accusing their possessors of some crime of which they were innocent, or by distorting their words into a free gift of their property to him. Many were convicted on these charges of murder and other crimes, and in order to escape paying the penalty for them, gave him all that they had. Some who were engaged in making frivolous claims to land belonging to their neighbours, when they found that they had no chance of winning their cause, as the law was against them, would make him a present of the land in dispute, and so get out of the difficulty. Thus they gained his favour by a gift that cost them nothing, and got the better of their adversaries by the most illegal means.

It will not be out of place, I think, to describe his personal appearance. He was neither tall nor too short, but of a medium height, not thin, but inclined to be fat. His face was round and not ill-favoured, and showed colour, even after a two days' fast. In a word, he greatly resembled Domitian, Vespasian's son, more than anybody else. This was the Emperor whom the Romans detested so much that they could not slake their hatred for him, even when they had torn him to pieces, but a decree of the Senate was passed to remove his name from all documents, and that all statues of him should be destroyed; wherefore his name has been erased from every inscription at Rome and everywhere else, except where it occurs in a list together with other emperors, and no statue of him is to be found in the Roman Empire, save one only, the history of which is as follows: Domitian had married a lady of noble birth and admirable conduct, who never harmed anyone, and always disapproved of her husband's evil deeds. As she was so much beloved, the Senate sent for her, after the death of Domitian, and bade her ask whatever favour she pleased. All that she asked was to receive Domitian's body for burial, and permission to erect a bronze statue to him in whatever place she might choose. The Senate consented, and Domitian's wife, not wishing to leave to posterity a memorial of the brutality of those who had butchered her husband, adopted the following plan. She collected the pieces of his body, pieced them accurately together, joined them properly, and sewed the body together again. She then sent for the statuaries, and bade them reproduce this pitiable object in a brazen statue. The workmen straightway made the statue, and his wife, having received it from them, set it up in the street which leads up to the Capitol from the Forum, on the right hand side, where to this day one may see Domitian's statue, showing the marks of his tragic end. One may say that the whole of Justinian's person, his expression, and all his features can be traced in this statue.

Such was his portrait; but it would be exceedingly difficult to give an accurate estimate of his character; he was an evil-doer, and yet easily led by the nose, being, in common parlance, a fool as well as a knave. He never was truthful with anyone, but always spoke and acted cunningly, yet any who chose could easily outwit him. His character was a sorry mixture of folly and bad principles. One may say of him what one of the Peripatetic philosophers of old said long ago, that in men, as in the mixing of colours, the most opposite qualities combine. I will therefore only describe his disposition as far as I have been able to fathom it.

This prince was deceitful, fond of crooked ways, artificial, given to hiding his wrath, double-faced, and cruel, exceedingly clever in concealing his thoughts, and never moved to tears either by joy or grief, but capable of weeping if the occasion required it. He was always a liar not merely on the spur of the moment; he drew up documents and swore the most solemn oaths to respect the covenants which he made with his subjects; then he would straightway break his plighted word and his oath, like the vilest of slaves, who perjure themselves and are only driven to confess through fear of torture. He was a faithless friend, an inexorable foe, and mad for murder and plunder; quarrelsome and revolutionary, easily led to do evil, never persuaded to act rightly, he was quick to contrive and carry out what was evil, but loathed even to hear of good actions.

How could any man fully describe Justinian's character? He had all these vices and other even greater ones, in larger proportion than any man; indeed, Nature seemed to have taken away all other men's vices and to have implanted them all in this man's breast. Besides all this, he was ever disposed to give ear to accusations, and quick to punish. He never tried a case before deciding it, but as soon as he had heard the plaintiff he straightway pronounced his judgment upon it. He wrote decrees, without the slightest hesitation, for the capture of fortresses, the burning of cities, the enslaving of whole races of men for no crime whatever, so that, if anyone were to reckon all the calamities of this nature which have befallen the Roman people before his time, and weigh them against those which were brought about by him, I imagine that it would be found that this man was guilty of far more bloodshed than any ruler of previous times.

He had no hesitation in coolly appropriating people's property, and did not even trouble himself to put forward any pretext or colourable legal ground for taking another man's goods; and, when he had got it, he was quite ready to squander it in foolish munificence or to spend it in unreasonable largesses to the barbarians. In fine, he neither had any property himself, nor would he suffer anyone else of all his subjects to have any; so that he did not seem to be so much governed by avarice as by jealousy of those who possessed wealth. He carelessly drove all the wealth of the Romans out of the country, and was the cause of general impoverishment. Such was the character of Justinian, as far as I am able to describe it.

CHAPTER IX

As for Justinian's wife, I shall now describe her birth, how she was brought up, how she married him, and how in conjunction with him she utterly ruined the Roman Empire.

There was one Acacius at Byzantium, of the Green faction, who was keeper of the wild beasts used in the amphitheatre, and was called the Bear-keeper. This man died of some malady during the reign of Anastasius, and left three daughters, Comito, Theodora and Anastasia, the eldest of whom was not yet seven years of age. His widow married her husband's successor in his house and profession; but the chief dancer of the Green faction, named Asterius, was easily bribed into taking away the office from this man and giving it to one who paid him for it: for the dancers had the power to manage these matters as they pleased.

When Theodora's mother saw the whole populace assembled in the amphitheatre to see the show of the wild beasts, she placed fillets on her daughters' heads and hands, and made them sit in the attitude of suppliants. The Greens regarded their appeal with indifference, but the Blues, who had lately lost their own bear-keeper, bestowed the office upon them. As the children grew up, their mother straightway sent them on the stage, for they were handsome girls. She did not send them on all at once, but as each one arrived at a fit age so to do. The eldest girl, Comito, had already become one of the most celebrated prostitutes of her time.

Theodora, the next eldest, was dressed in a little sleeved tunic, such as a slave-girl would wear, and waited on her sister, carrying on her shoulders the stool in which she was wont to sit in public. Theodora was still too young to have intercourse with a man after the manner of women, but she satisfied the unnatural passions of certain wretches, even the vilest slaves, who followed their masters to the theatre and amused their leisure by this infamy. She remained for some time also in a brothel, where she practised this hateful form of vice.

As soon, however, as she reached the age of puberty, as she was handsome, her mother sent her into the theatrical troupe, and she straightway became a simple harlot, as old-fashioned people called it; for she was neither a musician nor a dancer, but merely prostituted herself to everyone whom she met, giving up every part of her body to debauchery. She associated chiefly with the theatrical "pantomimes," and took part in their performances, playing in comic scenes, for she was exceedingly witty and amusing; so that she soon became well known by her acting. She had no shame whatever, and no one ever saw her put out of countenance, but she lent herself to scandalous purposes without the least hesitation.

She excelled in raising a laugh by being slapped on her puffed-out cheeks, and used to uncover herself so far as to show the spectators everything before and behind which decency forbids to be shown to men. She stimulated her lovers by lascivious jests, and continually invented new postures of coition, by which means she completely won the hearts of all libertines; for she did not wait to be solicited by anyone whom she met, but herself, with joke and gestures, invited everyone whom she fell in with, especially beardless boys.

She never succumbed to these transports; for she often went to a supper at which each one paid his share, with ten or more young men, in the full vigour of their age and practised in debauchery, and would pass the whole night with all of them. When they were all exhausted, she would go to their servants, thirty in number, it may be, and fornicate with each one of them; and yet not even so did she quench her lust. Once she went to the house of some great man, and while the guests were drinking pulled up her clothes on the edge of the couch and did not blush to exhibit her wantonness without reserve. Though she received the male in three orifices she nevertheless complained of Nature for not having made the passage of her breasts wider, that she might contrive a new form of coition in that part of her person also.

She frequently became pregnant, but as she employed all known remedies without delay, she promptly procured abortion. Often, even on the stage, she stripped before the eyes of all the people, and stood naked in their midst, wearing only a girdle about her private parts and groin; not because she had any modesty about showing that also to the people, but because no one was allowed to go on the stage without a girdle about those parts. In this attitude she would throw herself down on the floor, and lie on her back. Slaves, whose duty it was, would then pour grains of barley upon her girdle, which trained geese would then pick up with their beaks one by one and eat. She did not blush or rise up, but appeared to glory in this performance; for she was not only without shame, but especially fond of encouraging others to be shameless, and often would strip naked in the midst of the actors, and swing herself backwards and forwards, explaining to those who had already enjoyed her and those who had not, the peculiar excellences of that exercise.

She proceeded to such extremities of abuse as to make her face become what most women's private parts are: wherefore her lovers became known at once by their unnatural tastes, and any respectable man who met her in the public streets turned away, and made haste to avoid her, lest his clothes should be soiled by contact with such an abandoned creature, for she was a bird of ill-omen, especially for those who saw her early in the day. As for her fellow-actresses, she always abused them most savagely, for she was exceedingly jealous.

Afterwards she accompanied Hecebolus, who had received the appointment of Governor of Pentapolis, to that country, to serve his basest passions, but quarrelled with him, and was straightway sent out of the country. In consequence of this she fell into want of common necessaries, with which she hereafter provided herself by prostitution, as she had been accustomed to do. She first went to Alexandria, and afterwards wandered all through the East, until she reached Byzantium, plying her trade in every city on her way, a trade which, I imagine, Heaven will not pardon a man for calling by its right name, as if the powers of evil would not allow any place on earth to be free from the debaucheries of Theodora. Such was the birth, and such the training of this woman, and her name became better known than that of any other prostitute of her time.

On her return to Byzantium, Justinian became excessively enamoured of her. At first he had intercourse with her merely as her lover, although he raised her to the position of a patrician. By this means Theodora was straightway enabled to gain very great influence and to amass considerable sums of money. She charmed Justinian beyond all the world, and, like most infatuated lovers, he delighted to show her all the favour and give her all the money that he could. This lavishness added fuel to the flame of passion. In concert with her he plundered the people more than ever, not only in the capital, but throughout the Roman Empire; for, as both of them had for a long time been members of the Blue faction, they had placed unlimited power in its hands, although the evil was subsequently somewhat checked, in the manner which I will now relate.

Justinian had for some time suffered from a dangerous illness; in fact, it was even reported that he was dead. The Blue faction were committing the crimes of which I have spoken, and slew Hypatius, a person of consequence, in the Church of St. Sophia, in broad daylight. When the murderer had accomplished his work, clamour was raised which reached the Emperor's ears, and all his courtiers seized upon the opportunity of pointing out the outrageous character of the offence which, owing to Justinian's absence from public affairs, the murderer had been enabled to perpetrate, and enumerated all the crimes that had been committed from the outset. Hereupon the Emperor gave orders to the prefect of the city to punish these crimes. This man was named Theodotus, nick-named Colocynthius.[11] He instituted an inquiry into the whole matter, and had the courage to seize and put to death, according to the law, many of the malefactors, several of whom, however, hid themselves and so escaped, being destined to perish afterwards together with the Roman Empire. Justinian, who miraculously recovered, straightway began to plan the destruction of Theodotus, on the pretext that he was a magician and used philtres. However, as he found no proofs on which the man could be condemned, he flogged and tortured some of his intimates until he forced them to make most unfounded accusations against him. When no one dared to oppose Justinian, but silently bewailed the plot against Theodotus, Proclus, the Quaestor, alone declared that the man was innocent and did not deserve to die. Theodotus was therefore sentenced by the Emperor to banishment to Jerusalem. But, learning that certain men had been sent thither to assassinate him, he took sanctuary in the temple, where he spent the rest of his life in concealment until he died. Such was the end of Theodotus.

From this time forth, however, the Blue party behaved with the greatest moderation; they did not venture to perpetrate such crimes, although they had it in their power to abuse their authority more outrageously and with greater impunity than before. Here is a proof of this; when a few of them afterwards showed the same audacity in evil-doing, they were not punished in any way; for those who had the power to punish always gave malefactors an opportunity to escape, and by this indulgence encouraged them to trample upon the laws.

CHAPTER X

As long as the Empress Euphemia was alive, Justinian could not contrive to marry Theodora. Though she did not oppose him on any other point, she obstinately refused her consent to this one thing. She was altogether free from vice, although she was a homely person and of barbarian descent, as I have already said. She never cultivated any active virtues, but remained utterly ignorant of State affairs. She did not bear her own name, which was a ridiculous one, when she came to the palace, but was re-named Euphemia. Soon afterwards, however, she died.

Justin was in his second childhood and so sunk in senility that he was the laughing-stock of his subjects. All despised him utterly, and disregarded him because he was incompetent to control State affairs, but they paid their court to Justinian with awe, for he terrified them all by his love of disturbance and reckless innovations.

He then resolved to bring about his marriage with Theodora. It was forbidden by the most ancient laws of the State that anyone of the senatorial order should marry a courtesan; so he prevailed upon the Emperor to repeal the existing law and introduce a new one, whereby he was allowed to live with Theodora as his legitimate wife, and it became possible for anyone else to marry a courtesan. He also straightway assumed the demeanour of absolute despot, veiling his forcible seizure of power under the pretext of reasons of State. He was proclaimed Emperor of the Romans, as his uncle's colleague. Whether this was legal or not may be doubted, since he owed his election to the terror with which he inspired those who gave him their votes.

So Justinian and Theodora ascended the Imperial throne three days before Easter, at a time when it is forbidden to make visits or even to greet one's friends. A few days later Justin was carried off by disease, after a reign of nine years, and Justinian and Theodora reigned alone.

Thus did Theodora, as I have told you, in spite of her birth and bringing-up, reach the throne without finding any obstacle in her way. Justinian felt no shame at having wedded her, although he might have chosen the best born, the best educated, the most modest and virtuously nurtured virgin in all the Roman Empire, with outstanding breasts, as the saying is; whereas he preferred to take to himself the common refuse of all mankind, and without a thought of all that has been told, married a woman stained with the shame of many abortions and many other crimes. Nothing more, I conceive, need be said about this creature's character, for all the vices of his heart are thoroughly displayed in the fact of so unworthy a marriage. When a man feels no shame at an act of this kind, and braves the loathing of the world, there is thereafter no path of wickedness which may not be trodden by him, but, with a face incapable of blushing, he plunges, utterly devoid of scruple, into the deepest baseness.

However, no one in the Senate had the courage to show dissatisfaction at seeing the State fasten this disgrace upon itself, but all were ready to worship Theodora as if she had been a goddess. Neither did any of the clergy show any indignation, but bestowed upon her the title of "Lady." The people who had formerly seen her upon the stage now declared themselves, with uplifted hands, to be her slaves, and made no secret of the name. None of the army showed irritation at having to face the dangers of war in the service of Theodora, nor did anyone of all mankind offer her the least opposition. All, I suppose, yielded to circumstances, and suffered this disgraceful act to take place, as though Fortune had wished to display her power by disposing human affairs so that events came about in utter defiance of reason, and human counsel seemed to have no share in directing them. Fortune does thus raise men suddenly to great heights of power, by means in which reason has no share, in spite of all obstacles that may bar the way, for nothing can check her course, but she proceeds straight on towards her goal, and everything makes way for her. But let all this be, and be represented as it pleases God.

Theodora was at this time handsome and of a graceful figure, but she was short, without much colour, but rather of a pale complexion, and with brilliant and piercing eyes. It would take a life-time to tell of all her adventures during her theatrical life, but I think what little I have selected above will be sufficient to give an indication of her character. We must now briefly set forth what she and her husband did, for during their married life neither ever did anything without the other. For a long time they appeared to all to be at variance both in their characters and in their actions; but afterwards this disagreement was seen to have been purposely arranged between them, in order that their subjects might not come to an agreement and rise against them, but might all be divided in their opinion. First, they split up the Christians into two parties and brought them to ruin, as I shall tell you hereafter, by this plan of pretending to take different sides. Next they created divisions amongst the State factions. Theodora feigned to be an eager partisan of the Blues, and gave them permission to commit the greatest atrocities and deeds of violence against the opposite faction, while Justinian pretended to be grieved and annoyed in his secret soul, as though he could not oppose his wife's orders; and often they would pretend to act in opposition. The one would declare that the Blues must be punished because they were evil-doers, while the other pretended to be enraged, and angrily declared that she was overruled by her husband against her will. Yet, as I have said, the Blue faction seemed wondrously quiet, for they did not outrage their neighbours as much as they might have done.

In legal disputes, each of them would pretend to favour one of the litigants, and of necessity made the man with the worse case win; by this means they plundered both the parties of most of the disputed property. The Emperor received many persons into his intimacy, and gave them appointments with liberty to do what they pleased in the way of violent injustice and fraud against the State; but when they were seen to have amassed a considerable amount of wealth, they straightway fell into disgrace for having offended the Empress. At first Justinian would take upon himself to inquire kindly into their case, but soon he would drop the pretence of good-will, and his zeal on their behalf would throw the whole matter into confusion. Upon this, Theodora would treat them in the most shameful way, while he, pretending not to understand what was going on, would shamelessly confiscate their entire property. They used to carry on these machinations by appearing to be at variance, while really playing into each other's hands, and were thus able to set their subjects by their ears and firmly establish their own power.

CHAPTER XI

When Justinian came to the throne, he straightway succeeded in upsetting everything. What had previously been forbidden by the laws he introduced, while he abolished all existing institutions, as though he had assumed the imperial robe for no other purpose than to alter completely the form of government. He did away with existing offices, and established other new ones for the management of affairs. He acted in the same manner in regard to the laws and the army; not that he was led to do so by any love of justice or the public advantage, but merely in order that all institutions might be new and might bear his name; if there was any institution that he was unable to abolish at once, he gave it his name, that at least it might appear new. He could never satisfy his insatiable desire, either of money or blood; but after he had plundered one wealthy house, he would seek for another to rob, and straightway squander the plunder upon subsidies to barbarians, or senseless extravagance in building. After he had destroyed his victims by tens of thousands, he immediately began to lay plots against even greater numbers. As the Roman Empire was at peace with foreign nations, his impatience of quiet led him, out of uncontrollable love of bloodshed, to set the barbarians fighting with one another. Sending for the chieftains of the Huns for no reason whatever, he took a pride in lavishing great sums of money upon them, under the pretext of securing their friendship, just as he did in the time of the Emperor Justin, as I have already told you. These Huns, when they had got the money, sent to some of their fellow-chieftains with their retainers, and bade them make inroads into the Emperor's territory, that they also might make a bargain with him for the peace which he was so ready to purchase. These men straightway subjugated the Empire, and nevertheless remained in the

Emperor's pay; and, following their examples, others straightway began to harass the wretched Romans, and, after they had secured their booty, were graciously rewarded by the Emperor for their invasion. Thus the whole Hunnish nation, one tribe after another, never ceased at any time to lay waste and plunder the Empire; for these barbarians are under several independent chieftains, and the war, having once begun through his foolish generosity, never came to an end, but always kept beginning anew; so that, during this time, there was no mountain, no cave, no spot whatever in the Roman Empire that remained unravaged, and many countries were harried and plundered by the enemy more than five several times.

These calamities, and those which were brought upon the Empire by the Medes, the Saracens, the Sclavonians, the Antes, and other barbarians, I have described in the previous books of my history; but, as I have said at the beginning of this story, I was here obliged to explain the causes which led thereto.

Justinian paid Chosroes many centenars in order to secure peace, and then, with unreasonable arbitrariness, did more than anyone to break the truce, by employing every effort to bring Alamundur and his Huns over to his own side, as I have already set forth in plain terms in my history.

While he was stirring up all this strife and war to plague the Romans, he also endeavoured, by various devices, to drench the earth in human blood, to carry off more riches for himself, and to murder many of his subjects. He proceeded as follows. There prevail in the Roman Empire many Christian doctrines which are known as heresies, such as those of the Montanists and Sabbatians and all the others by which men's minds are led astray. Justinian ordered all these beliefs to be abandoned in favour of the old religion, and threatened the recusants with legal disability to transmit their property to their wives and children by will. The churches of these so-called heretics, especially those belonging to the Arian heresy, were rich beyond belief. Neither the whole of the Senate, or any other of the greatest corporations in the Roman Empire, could be compared with these churches in wealth. They had gold and silver plate and jewels more than any man could count or describe; they owned many mansions and villages, and large estates everywhere, and everything else which is reckoned and called wealth among men.

As none of the previous Emperors had interfered with them, many people, even of the orthodox faith, procured, through this wealth, work and the means of livelihood. But the Emperor Justinian first of all sequestrated all the property of these churches, and suddenly took away all that they possessed, by which many people lost the means of subsistence. Many agents were straightway sent out to all parts of the Empire to force whomsoever they met to change the faith of his forefathers. These homely people, considering this an act of impiety, decided to oppose the Emperor's agents. Hereupon many were put to death by the persecuting faction, and many made an end of themselves, thinking, in their superstitious folly, that this course best satisfied the claims of religion; but the greater part of them voluntarily quitted the land of their forefathers, and went into exile. The Montanists, who were settled in Phrygia, shut themselves up in their churches, set them on fire, and perished in the flames; and, from this time forth, nothing was to be seen in the Roman Empire except massacres and flight.

Justinian straightway passed a similar law with regard to the Samaritans, which produced a riot in Palestine. In my own city of Caesarea and other cities, the people, thinking that it was a foolish thing to suffer for a mere senseless dogma, adopted, in place of the name which they had hitherto borne, the appellation of "Christians," and so avoided the danger with which they were threatened by this law. Such of them as had any claims to reason and who belonged to the better class, thought it their duty to remain stedfast to their new faith; but the greater part, as though out of pique at having been forced against their will by the law to abandon the faith of their fathers, adopted the belief of the Manicheans, or what is known as Polytheism.

But all the country people met together in a body and determined to take up arms against the Emperor. They chose a leader of their own, named Julian, the son of Sabarus, and for some time held their own in the struggle with the Imperial troops, but were at last defeated and cut to pieces, together with their leader. It is said that one hundred thousand men fell in this engagement, and the most fertile country on the earth has ever since been without cultivators. This did great harm to the Christian landowners in that country, for, although they received nothing from their property, yet they were forced to pay heavy taxes yearly to the Emperor for the rest of their lives, and no abatement or relief from this burden was granted to them.

After this he began to persecute those who were called Gentiles, torturing their persons and plundering their property. All of these people, who decided to adopt the Christian faith nominally, saved themselves for the time, but not long afterwards most of them were caught offering libations and sacrifices and performing other unholy rites. How he treated the Christians I will subsequently relate.

Next he forbade paederasty by law, and he made this law apply not only to those who transgressed it after it had been passed, but even to those who had practised this wickedness long before. The law was applied to these persons in the loosest fashion, the testimony of one man or boy, who possibly might be a slave unwilling to bear witness against his master, was held to be sound evidence. Those who were convicted were carried through the city, after having had their genitals cut off. This cruelty was not at first practised against any except those who belonged to the Green faction or were thought to be very rich, or had otherwise offended.

Justinian and Theodora also dealt very harshly with the astrologers, so that the officers appointed to punish thieves proceeded against these men for no other cause than that they were astrologers, dealt many stripes on their backs, and paraded them on camels through the city; yet they were old and respectable men, against whom no reproach could be brought except that they dwelt in Byzantium and were learned about the stars.

There was a continual stream of emigration, not only to the lands of the barbarians, but also to the nations most remote from Rome; and one saw a very great number of foreigners both in the country and in each city of the Empire, for men lightly exchanged their native land for another, as though their own country had been captured by an enemy.

CHAPTER XII

Those who were considered the wealthiest persons in Byzantium and the other cities of the Empire, next after members of the Senate, were robbed of their wealth by Justinian and Theodora in the manner which I have described above. I shall now describe how they managed to take away all the property of members of the Senate.

There was at Constantinople one Zeno, the grandson of that Anthemius who formerly had been Emperor of the West. They sent this man to Egypt as governor. He delayed his departure, while he loaded his ship with precious valuables; for he had silver beyond any man's counting, and gold plate set with pearls and emeralds, and with other like precious stones. But Justinian and Theodora bribed some of those who passed for his most faithful servants, to take everything out of the ship as fast as they could, set it on fire in the hold, and then go and tell Zeno that his ship had taken fire of its own accord, and that all his property was lost. Some time after this Zeno died suddenly, and they took possession of his property as his heirs, producing a will which, it is currently reported, was never made by him.

In like manner they made themselves the heirs of Tatian, of Demosthenes, and of Hilara, persons who at that time held the first rank in the Roman Senate. They obtained other persons' fortunes by the production, not of formal wills, but of counterfeit conveyances. This was how they became the heirs of Dionysius, who dwelt in Libanus, and of John the son of Basil, who was the leading man in Edessa, and had been delivered up to the Persians as a hostage against his will by Belisarius, as I have told already. Chosroes kept this John a prisoner, and refused to let him go, declaring that the Romans had not performed all the terms of the treaty for which John had been given in pledge by Belisarius, but he was prepared to let him be ransomed as a prisoner of war. His grandmother, who was still alive, got together the money for his ransom, not less than two thousand pounds of silver, and would have ransomed her grandson; but when this money arrived at Dara, the Emperor heard of the transaction and forbade it, that the wealth of Romans might not be conveyed to barbarians. Not long after this John fell ill and died; whereupon the governor of the city forged a letter which he said John had written to him as a friend not long before, to the effect that he desired the Emperor to succeed to his property.

I could not give the list of all the other people whose heirs Justinian and Theodora became by the free will of the testators. However, up to the time of the insurrection called Nika, they only plundered rich men of their property one by one; but when this broke out, as I have described in my former works, they then sequestrated nearly all the property of the Senate. They laid their hands upon all movables and the finest parts of the estates, but set apart such lands as were burdened with grievous imposts, and, under pretence of kindness, restored them to their former possessors. So these people, oppressed by the tax-gatherers, and tormented by the never-ceasing interest to be paid upon their debts, became weary of their lives.

For the reasons which I have stated, I, and many of my position, never believed that they were really two human beings, but evil demons, and what the poets call scourges of mankind, who laid their heads together to see how they could fastest and most easily destroy the race and the works of man, but who had assumed human forms, and become something between men and demons, and thus convulsed the whole world. One can find proofs of this theory more particularly in the superhuman power with which they acted.

There is a wide distinction between the human and the supernatural. Many men have been born in every age who, either by circumstances or their own character, have shown themselves terrible beings, who became the ruin of cities, countries, and whatever else fell into their hands; but to destroy all men and to ruin the whole earth has been granted to none save these two, who have been helped by Fortune in their schemes to destroy the whole human race. For, about this time, much ruin was caused by earthquakes, pestilences and inundations of rivers, as I shall immediately tell you. Thus it was not by mere human power, but by something greater, that they were enabled to work their evil will.

It is said that Justinian's mother told some of her intimates that Justinian was not the son of Sabbatius, her husband, or of any human being; but that, at the time when she became pregnant, an unseen demon companied with her, whom she only felt as when a man has connection with a woman, and who then vanished away as in a dream.

Some who have been in Justinian's company in the palace very late at night, men with a clear conscience, have thought that in his place they have beheld a strange and devilish form. One of them said that Justinian suddenly arose from his royal throne and walked about (although, indeed, he never could sit still for long), and that at that moment his head disappeared, while the rest of his body still seemed to move to and fro. The man who beheld this stood trembling and troubled in mind, not knowing how to believe his eyes. Afterwards the head joined the body again, and united itself to the parts from which it had so strangely been severed.

Another declared that he stood beside Justinian as he sat, and of a sudden his face turned into a shapeless mass of flesh, without either eyebrows or eyes in their proper places, or anything else which makes a man recognisable; but after a while he saw the form of his face come back again. What I write here I did not see myself, but I heard it told by men who were positive that they had seen it.

They say, too, that a certain monk, highly in favour with God, was sent to Byzantium by those who dwelt with him in the desert, to beg that favour might be shown to their neighbours, who had been wronged and outraged beyond endurance. When he arrived at Byzantium, he straightway obtained an audience of the Emperor; but just as he was about to enter his apartment, he started back, and, turning round, suddenly withdrew. The eunuch, who was escorting him, and also the bystanders, besought him earnestly to go forward, but he made no answer, but like one who has had a stroke of the palsy, made his way back to his lodging. When those who had come with him asked why he acted thus, they say that he distinctly stated that he saw the chief of the devils sitting on his throne in the midst of the palace, and he would not meet him or ask anything of him. How can one believe this man to have been anything but an evil demon, who never took his fill of drink, food, or sleep, but snatched at the meals which were set before him anyhow, and roamed about the palace at untimely hours of the night, and yet was so passionately addicted to venery.

Some of Theodora's lovers, when she was still on the stage, declare that a demon had fallen upon them and driven them out of her bedchamber that it might pass the night with her. There was a dancer named Macedonia, who belonged to the Blue faction at Antioch, and had very great influence with Justinian. This woman used to write letters to him while Justin was still on the throne, and thus easily made away with any great man in the East whom she chose, and caused their property to be confiscated for the public use. They say that this Macedonia once greeted Theodora, when she saw her very much troubled and cast down at the ill-treatment which she had received at the hands of Hecebolius, and at the loss of her money on her journey, and encouraged and cheered her, bidding her remember the fickleness of fortune, which might again grant her great possessions. They say that Theodora used to tell how, that night, she had a dream which bade her take no thought about money, for that when she came to Byzantium, she would share the bed of the chief of the demons; that she must manage by all means to become his wedded wife, and that afterwards she would have all the wealth of the world at her disposal.

This was the common report in regard to these matters.

CHAPTER XIII

Although Justinian's character was such as I have already explained, he was easy of access, and affable to those whom he met. No one was ever denied an audience, and he never was angry even with those who did not behave or speak properly in his presence. But, on the other hand, he never felt ashamed of any of the murders which he committed. However, he never displayed any anger or pettishness against those who offended him, but preserved a mild countenance and an unruffled brow, and with a gentle voice would order tens of thousands of innocent men to be put to death, cities to be taken by storm, and property to be confiscated. One would think, from his manner, that he had the character of a sheep; but if anyone, pitying his victims, were to endeavour, by prayers and supplications, to make him relent, he would straightway become savage, show his teeth, and vent his rage upon his subjects. As for the priests, he let them override their neighbours with impunity, and delighted to see them plunder those round about them, thinking that in this manner he was showing piety. Whenever he had to decide any lawsuit of this sort, he thought that righteous judgment consisted in letting the priest win his cause and leave the court in triumph with some plunder to which he had no right whatever; for, to him, justice meant the success of the priest's cause. He himself, when by malpractices he had obtained possession of the property of people, alive or dead, would straightway present his plunder to one of the churches, by which means he would hide his rapacity under the cloak of piety, and render it impossible for his victims ever to recover their possessions. Indeed, he committed numberless murders through his notion of piety; for, in his zeal to bring all men to agree in one form of Christian doctrine, he recklessly murdered all who dissented therefrom, under the pretext of piety, for he did not think that it was murder, if those whom he slew were not of the same belief as himself. Thus, his thoughts were always fixed upon slaughter, and, together with his wife, he neglected no excuse which could bring it about; for both of these beings had for the most part the same passions, but sometimes they played a part which was not natural to them; for each of them was thoroughly wicked, and by their pretended differences of opinion, brought their subjects to ruin. Justinian's character was weaker than water, and anyone could lead him whither he would, provided it was not to commit any act of kindness or incur the loss of money. He especially delighted in flattery, so that his flatterers could easily make him believe that he should soar aloft and tread upon the clouds. Once indeed, Tribonianus, when sitting by him, declared that he was afraid that some day Justinian would be caught up into heaven because of his righteousness, and would be lost to men. Such praises, or rather sneers, as these he constantly bore in mind; yet, if he admired any man for his goodness, he would shortly afterwards upbraid him for a villain, and after having railed at one of his subjects without any cause, he would suddenly take to praising him, having changed his mind on no grounds whatever; for what he really thought was always the opposite of what he said, and wished to appear to think. How he was affected by emotions of love or hate I think I have sufficiently indicated by what I have said concerning his actions. As an enemy, he was obstinate and relentless; as a friend, inconstant; for he made away with many of his strongest partisans, but never became the friend of anyone whom he had once disliked. Those whom he appeared to consider his nearest and dearest friends he would in a short time deliver up to ruin to please his wife or anyone else, although he knew well that they died only because of devotion for him; for he was untrustworthy in all things save cruelty and avarice, from which nothing could restrain him. Whenever his wife could not persuade him to do a thing, she used to suggest that great gain was likely to result from it, and this enabled her to lead him into any course of action against his will. He did not blush to make laws and afterwards repeal them, that he might make some infamous profit thereby. Nor did he give judgment according to the laws which he himself had made, but in favour of the side which promised him the biggest and most splendid bribe. He thought it no disgrace to steal away the property of his subjects, little by little, in cases where he had no grounds for taking it away all at one swoop, either by some unexpected charge or a forged will. While he was Emperor of the Romans neither faith in God nor religion was secure, no law continued in force, no action, no contract was binding. When he intrusted any business to his officials, if they put to death numbers of those who fell into their hands and carried off great wealth as plunder, they were looked upon as faithful servants of the Emperor, and were spoken of as men who had accurately carried out his instructions; but, if they came back after having shown any mercy, he took a dislike to them and was their enemy for life, and never again would employ them, being disgusted with their old-fashioned ways. For this reason many men were anxious to prove to him that they were villains, although they really were not such. He would often make men repeated promises, and confirm his promise by an oath or by writing, and then purposely forget all about it, and think that such an action did him credit. Justinian behaved in this manner not only towards his own subjects, but also towards many of his enemies, as I have already told. As a rule he dispensed with both rest and sleep, and never took his fill of either food or drink, but merely picked up a morsel to taste with the tips of his fingers, and then left his dinner, as if eating had been a bye-work imposed upon him by nature. He would often go without food for two days and nights, especially when fasting was enjoined, on the eve of the feast of Easter, when he would often fast for two days, taking no sustenance beyond a little water and a few wild herbs, and sleeping, as it might be, for one hour only, passing the rest of the time in walking to and fro. Had he spent all this time in useful works, the State would have nourished exceedingly; but, as it was, he used his natural powers to work the ruin of the Romans, and succeeded in thoroughly disorganizing the constitution. His constant wakefulness, his privations, and his labour were undergone for no other purpose than to make the sufferings of his subjects every day more grievous; for, as I have said before, he was especially quick in devising crimes, and swift to carry them out, so that even his good qualities seemed to have been so largely bestowed upon him merely for the affliction of his people.

CHAPTER XIV

Everything was done at the wrong time, and nothing that was established was allowed to continue. To prevent my narrative being interminable, I will merely mention a few instances, and pass over the remainder in silence. In the first place, Justinian neither possessed in himself the appearance of Imperial dignity, nor demanded that it should be respected by others, but imitated the barbarians in language, appearance, and ideas. When he had to issue an Imperial decree, he did not intrust it to the Quaestor in the usual way, but for the most part delivered it himself by word of mouth, although he spoke his own language like a foreigner; or else he left it in the hands of one of those by whom he was surrounded, so that those who had been injured by such resolutions did not know to whom to apply. Those who were called A Secretis,[12] and had from very ancient times fulfilled the duty of writing the secret dispatches of the Emperor, were no longer allowed to retain their privileges; for he himself wrote them nearly all, even the sentences of the municipal magistrates, no one throughout the Roman world being permitted to administer justice with a free hand. He took everything upon himself with unreasoning arrogance, and so managed cases that were to be decided, that, after he had heard one of the litigants, he immediately pronounced his verdict and obliged them to submit to it, acting in accordance with no law or principle of justice, but being evidently overpowered by shameful greed. For the Emperor was not ashamed to take bribes, since his avarice had deprived him of all feelings of shame. It frequently happened that the decrees of the Senate and the edicts of the Emperor were opposed to each other; for the Senate was as it were but an empty shadow, without the power of giving its vote or of keeping up its dignity; it was assembled merely for form's sake and in order to keep up an ancient custom, for none of its members were allowed to utter a single word. But the Emperor and his consort took upon themselves the consideration of questions that were to be discussed, and whatever resolutions they came to between themselves prevailed. If he whose cause had been victorious had any doubt as to the legality of his success, all he had to do was to make a present of gold to the Emperor, who immediately promulgated a law contrary to all those formerly in force. If, again, anyone else desired the revival of the law that had been repealed, the autocrat did not disdain to revoke the existing order of things and to re-establish it. There was nothing stable in his authority, but the balance of justice inclined to one side or the other, according to the weight of gold in either scale. In the market-place there were buildings under the management of palace officials, where traffic was carried on, not only in judicial, but also in legislative decisions. The officers called "Referendars" (or mediators) found it difficult to present the requests of petitioners to the Emperor, and still more difficult to bring before the council in the usual manner the answer proper to be made to each of them; but, gathering together from all quarters worthless and false testimony, they deceived Justinian, who was naturally a fit subject for deception, by fallacious reports and misleading statements. Then, immediately going out to the contending parties, without acquainting them with the conversation that had taken place, they extorted from them as much money as they required, without anyone venturing to oppose them.

Even the soldiers of the Praetorian guard, whose duty it was to attend the judges in the court of the palace, forced from them whatsoever judgments they pleased. All, so to speak, abandoned their own sphere of duty, and followed the paths that pleased them, however difficult or untrodden they had previously been. Everything was out of gear; offices were degraded, not even their names being preserved. In a word, the Empire resembled a queen over boys at play. But I must pass over the rest, as I hinted at the commencement of this work.

I will now say something about the man who first taught the Emperor to traffic in the administration of justice. His name was Leo; he was a native of Cilicia, and passionately eager to enrich himself. He was the most utterly shameless of flatterers, and most apt in ingratiating himself with the ignorant, and with the Emperor, whose folly he made use of in order to ruin his subjects. It was this Leo who first persuaded Justinian to barter justice for money. When this man had once discovered these means of plunder, he never stopped. The evil spread and reached such a height that, if anyone desired to come off victorious in an unjust cause against an honest man, he immediately repaired to Leo, and, promising to give half of his claim to be divided between the latter and the Emperor, left the palace, having already gained his cause, contrary to all principles of right and justice. In this manner Leo acquired a vast fortune, and a great quantity of land, and became the chief cause of the ruin of the State. There was no longer any security in contracts, in law, in oaths, in written documents, in any penalty agreed upon, or in any other security, unless money had been previously given to Leo and the Emperor. Nor was even this method certain, for Justinian would accept bribes from both parties; and, after having drained the pockets of both of those who had put confidence in him, he was not ashamed to cheat one or other of them (no matter which), for, in his eyes, there was nothing disgraceful in playing a double part, provided only that it turned out profitable for him.

Such a man was Justinian.

CHAPTER XV

As for Theodora, her disposition was governed by the most hardened and inveterate cruelty. She never did anything either under persuasion or compulsion, but employed all her self-willed efforts to carry out her resolutions, and no one ventured to intercede in favour of those who fell in her way. Neither length of time, nor fulness of punishment, nor carefully drawn-up prayers, nor the fear of death, nor the vengeance of Heaven, by awe of which the whole human race is impressed, could persuade her to abate her wrath. In a word, no one ever saw Theodora reconciled to one who had offended her, either during his lifetime or after his death; for the children of the deceased father inherited the hatred of the Empress, as if it were part of his patrimony; and, when he died, left it in turn to his sons. Her mind was ever most readily stirred to the destruction of men, and was incapable of being checked. She bestowed upon her person greater care than necessity demanded, but less than her desire prompted her to. She entered the bath very early in the morning; and, having spent a long time over her ablutions, went to breakfast, and afterwards again retired to rest. At dinner and supper she partook of every kind of food and drink. She slept a great deal: during the day, till nightfall, and, during the night, till sunrise. And, although she thus abandoned herself to every intemperance, she considered that the little time she had left was sufficient for the conduct of the affairs of the Roman Empire. If the Emperor intrusted anyone with a commission without having previously consulted Theodora, the unfortunate man soon found himself deprived of his office, in the deepest disgrace, and perished by a most dishonourable death. Justinian was speedy in the conduct of business of all kinds, not only owing to his continual sleeplessness (as has been mentioned before), but also by reason of his easiness of temper, and, above all, his affability. For he allowed people to approach him, although they were altogether obscure and unknown; and the interview was not limited to mere admission to the presence of the Emperor, but he permitted them to converse and associate with him on confidential terms. With the Empress the case was different; even the highest officials were not admitted until they had waited a long time, and after a great deal of trouble. They all waited patiently every day, like so many slaves, in a body, in a narrow and stifling room; for the risk they ran if they absented themselves was most serious. There they remained standing all the time on tip-toe, each trying to keep his face above his fellow's, that the eunuchs, as they came out, might see them. Some were invited to her presence, but rarely, and after several days of attendance; when at last they were admitted, they merely did obeisance to her, kissed both her feet, and then hastily retired in great awe; for they were not allowed to address her or to prefer any request except at her bidding; so slavishly had the spirit of Roman society degenerated under the instruction of Theodora, and to such a state of decay had the affairs of the Empire sunk, partly in consequence of the too great apparent easiness of the Emperor, partly owing to the harsh and peevish nature of Theodora; for the easiness of the one was uncertain, while the peevishness of the other hindered the transaction of public business.

There was this difference in their disposition and manner of life; but, in their love of money, thirst of blood, and aversion to truth, they were in perfect accord. They were, both of them, exceedingly clever inventors of falsehoods; if any one of those who had incurred the displeasure of Theodora was accused of any offence, however trivial and unimportant, she immediately trumped up against him charges with which he was in no way concerned, and greatly aggravated the matter. A number of accusations were heard, and a court was immediately appointed to put down and plunder the subjects; judges were called together by her, who would compete amongst themselves to see which of them might best be able to accommodate his decision to the cruelty of Theodora. The property of the accused was immediately confiscated, after he had first been cruelly flogged by her orders (although he might be descended from an illustrious family), nor had she any scruples about banishing, or even putting him to death. On the other hand, if any of her favourites were found guilty of murder or any other great crime, she pulled to pieces and scoffed at the efforts of the accusers, and forced them, against their will, to abandon proceedings. Whenever it pleased her, she turned affairs of the greatest importance into ridicule, as if they were taking place upon the stage of the theatre. A certain patrician, of advanced age, and who had for a long time held office (whose name is known to me, although I will not disclose it, in order to avoid bringing infinite disgrace upon him), being unable to recover a large sum of money which was owing to him from one of Theodora's attendants, applied to her, intending to press his claim against the debtor, and to beg her to assist him in obtaining his rights. Having heard of this beforehand, Theodora ordered her eunuchs to surround the patrician in a body on his arrival, and to listen to what was said by her, so that they might reply in a set form of words previously suggested by her. When the patrician entered her chamber, he prostrated himself at her feet in the usual manner, and, with tears in his eyes, thus addressed her:

"O sovereign lady! it is hard for a patrician to be in want of money; for that which in the case of others excites pity and compassion, becomes, in the case of a person of rank, a calamity and a disgrace. When any ordinary individual is in great straits, and informs his creditors, this immediately affords him relief from his trouble; but a patrician, when unable to pay his creditors, would, in the first place, be ashamed to own it; and, if he did so, he would never make them believe it, since the world is firmly convinced that poverty can never be associated with our class; even if he should persuade them to believe it, it would be the greatest blow to his dignity and reputation that could happen. Well, my lady, I owe money to some, while others owe money to me. Out of respect for my rank, I cannot cheat my creditors, who are pressing me sorely, whereas my debtors, not being patricians, have recourse to cruel subterfuges. Wherefore, I beg and entreat and implore your majesty to assist me to gain my rights, and to deliver me from my present misfortunes!"

Such were his words. Theodora then commenced to sing, "O patrician," and the eunuchs took up her words and joined in chorus, "you have a large tumour." When he again entreated her, and added a few words to the same effect as before, her only answer was the same refrain, which was taken up by the chorus of eunuchs. At length the unhappy man, tired of the whole affair, did reverence to the Empress in the usual manner, and returned home.

During the greater part of the year, Theodora resided in the suburbs on the coast, chiefly in the Heraeum, where her numerous retinue and attendants suffered great inconvenience, for they were short of the necessaries of life, and were exposed to the perils of the sea, of sudden storms, or the attacks of sea-monsters. However, they regarded the greatest misfortunes as of no importance, if only they had the means of enjoying the pleasures of the court.

CHAPTER XVI

I will now relate how Theodora treated those who had offended her, merely giving a few details, that I may not seem to have undertaken a task without end.

When Amalasunta, as I have narrated in the earlier books, desiring to abandon her connection with the affairs of the Goths, resolved to change her manner of life, and to retire to Byzantium, Theodora, considering that she was of illustrious descent and a princess, that she was of singular beauty, and exceedingly active in forming plans to carry out her wishes, was seized with suspicion of her distinguished qualities and eminent courage, and at the same time with apprehensions on account of her husband's fickleness. This made her exceedingly jealous; and she determined to compass the death of her rival by intrigue. She immediately persuaded the Emperor to send a man named Peter, by himself, to Italy, as ambassador to her. On his setting out, the Emperor gave him the instructions which I have mentioned in the proper place, where it was impossible for me to inform my readers of the truth, for fear of the Empress. The only order she gave the ambassador was to compass the death of Amalasunta with all possible despatch, having bribed him with the promise of great rewards if he successfully carried out his instructions. This man, expecting either preferment or large sums of money (for under such circumstances men are not slow to commit an unjust murder), when he reached Italy, by some arguments or other persuaded Theodatus to make away with Amalasunta. After this, Peter was advanced to the dignity of "Master of Offices," and attained to the highest influence, in spite of the detestation with which he was universally regarded. Such was the end of the unhappy Amalasunta.

Justinian had a secretary named Priscus, a Paphlagonian by birth, a man distinguished in every kind of villainy, a likely person to please the humour of his master, to whom he was exceedingly devoted, and from whom he expected to receive similar consideration; and by these means, in a short time, he unjustly amassed great wealth. Theodora, unable to endure his insolence and opposition, accused him to the Emperor. At first she was unsuccessful, but, shortly afterwards, she put him on board a ship, sent him away to a place she had previously determined upon, and having ordered him to be shaved, forced him to become a priest. In the meantime, Justinian, pretending that he knew nothing of what was going on, neither inquired to what part of the world Priscus had been banished, nor ever thought of him again afterwards, but remained silent, as if he had fallen into a state of lethargy. However, he seized the small fortune that he had left behind him.

Theodora had become suspicious of one of her servants named Areobindus, a barbarian by birth, but a youth of great comeliness, whom she had appointed her steward. Wishing to purge the imagined offence, (although, as was said) she was violently enamoured of him, she caused him to be cruelly beaten with rods, for no apparent reason. What became of him afterwards we do not know; nor has anyone seen him up to the present day. For when Theodora desired to keep any of her actions secret, she took care to prevent their being talked about or remembered. None of those who were privy to them were permitted to disclose them even to their nearest relations, or to any who desired to obtain information on the subject, however curious they might be. No tyrant had ever yet inspired such fear, since it was impossible for any word or deed of her opponents to pass unnoticed. For she had a number of spies in her employ who informed her of everything that was said and done in public places and private houses. When she desired to punish anyone who had offended her, she adopted the following plan. If he were a patrician, she sent for him privately, and handed him over to one of her confidential attendants, with instructions to carry him to the furthest boundaries of the empire. In the dead of night, her agent, having bound the unfortunate man and muffled his face, put him on board a ship, and, having accompanied him to the place whither he had been instructed to convey him, departed, having first delivered him secretly to another who was experienced in this kind of service, with orders that he was to be kept under the strictest watch, and that no one should be informed of it, until either the Empress took pity upon the unfortunate man, or, worn out by his sufferings, he at length succumbed and died a miserable death.

A youth of distinguished family, belonging to the Green faction, named Basianus, had incurred the Empress's displeasure by speaking of her in sarcastic terms. Hearing that she was incensed against him, he fled for refuge to the church of St. Michael the Archangel. Theodora immediately sent the Praetor of the people to seize him, bidding him charge him, however, not with insolence towards herself, but with the crime of sodomy. The magistrate, having dragged him from the church, subjected him to such intolerable torments, that the whole assembled people, deeply moved at seeing a person of such noble mien, and one who had been so delicately brought up, exposed to such shameful treatment, immediately commiserated his sufferings, and cried out with loud lamentations that reached the heavens, imploring pardon for the young man. But Theodora persisted in her work of punishment, and caused his death by ordering him to be castrated, although he had been neither tried nor condemned. His property was confiscated by the Emperor. Thus this woman, when infuriated, respected neither the sanctuary of the church, nor the prohibitive authority of the laws, nor the intercession of the people, nor any other obstacle whatsoever. Nothing was able to save from her vengeance anyone who had given her offence. She conceived a hatred, on the ground of his belonging to the Green faction, for a certain Diogenes, a native of Constantinople, an agreeable person, who was liked by the Emperor and everyone else. In her wrath, she accused him, in like manner, of sodomy, and, having suborned two of his servants, put them up to give evidence against and to accuse their master. But, as he was not tried secretly and in private, as was the usual custom, but in public, owing to the reputation he enjoyed, a number of distinguished persons were selected as judges, and they, scrupulous in the discharge of their duties, rejected the testimony of his servants as insufficient, especially on the ground of their not being of legal age. The Empress thereupon caused one of the intimate friends of Diogenes, named Theodorus, to be shut up in one of her ordinary prisons, and endeavoured to win him over, at one time by flattery, at another by ill-treatment. When none of these measures proved successful, she ordered a cord of ox-hide to be bound round his head, over his forehead and ears and then to be twisted and tightened. She expected that, under this treatment, his eyes would have started from their sockets, and that he would have lost his sight. But Theodorus refused to tell a lie. The judges, for want of proof, acquitted him; and his acquittal was made the occasion of public rejoicing.

Such was the manner in which Theodorus was treated.

CHAPTER XVII

As for the manner in which she treated Belisarius, Photius, and Buzes, I have already spoken of it at the commencement of this work.

Two Cilicians, belonging to the Blue faction, during a mutiny, laid violent hands upon Callinicus, governor of the second Cilicia, and slew his groom, who was standing near him, and endeavoured to defend his master, in the presence of the governor and all the people. Callinicus condemned them to death, since they had been convicted of several other murders besides this. When Theodora heard of this, in order to show her devotion to the party of the Blues, she ordered that the governor, while he still held office, should be crucified in the place where the two offenders had been executed, although he had committed no crime. The Emperor, pretending that he bitterly lamented his loss, remained at home, grumbling and threatening all kinds of vengeance upon the perpetrators of the deed. He did nothing, however; but, without scruple, appropriated the property of the dead man to his own use. Theodora likewise devoted her attention to punishing those women who prostituted their persons. She collected more than five hundred harlots, who sold themselves for three obols in the market-place, thereby securing a bare subsistence, and transported them to the other side of the Bosphorus, where she shut them up in the Monastery of Repentance, with the object of forcing them to change their manner of life. Some of them, however, threw themselves from the walls during the night, and in this manner escaped a change of life so contrary to their inclinations.

There were at Byzantium two young sisters, illustrious not only by the consulships of their father and grandfather, but by a long descent of nobility, and belonging to one of the chief families of the Senate. They had married early and lost their husbands. Theodora, charging them with living an immoral life, selected two debauchees from the common people and designed to make them their husbands. The young widows, fearing that they might be forced to obey, took refuge in the church of St. Sophia, and, approaching the sacred bath, clung closely to the font. But the Empress inflicted such privations and cruel treatment upon them, that they preferred marriage in order to escape from their immediate distress. In this manner Theodora showed that she regarded no sanctuary as inviolable, no spot as sacred. Although suitors of noble birth were ready to espouse these ladies, they were married against their will to two men, poor and outcast, and far below them in rank. Their mother, who was a widow like themselves, was present at the marriage, but did not venture to cry out or express her sorrow at this atrocious act. Afterwards, Theodora, repenting of what she had done, endeavoured to console them by promoting their husbands to high offices to the public detriment. But even this was no consolation to these young women, for their husbands inflicted incurable and insupportable woes upon almost all their subjects, as I will describe later; for Theodora paid no heed to the dignity of the office, the interests of the State, or any other consideration, provided only she could accomplish her wishes.

While still on the stage, she became with child by one of her friends, but did not perceive her misfortune until it was too late. She tried all the means she had formerly employed to procure abortion, but she was unable prematurely to destroy the living creature by any means whatsoever, since it had nearly assumed the form of a human being. Therefore, finding her remedies unsuccessful, she abandoned the attempt, and was obliged to bring forth the child. Its father, seeing that Theodora was at a loss what to do, and was indignant because, now that she had become a mother, she was no longer able to traffic with her person as before, and being with good reason in fear for the child's life, took it up, named it John, and carried it away with him to Arabia, whither he had resolved to retire. The father, just before his death, gave John, who was now grown up, full information concerning his mother.

John, having performed the last offices for his dead father, some time afterwards repaired to Byzantium, and explained the state of affairs to those who were charged with the duty of arranging admission to an audience with the Empress. They, not suspecting that she would conceive any inhuman designs against him, announced to the mother the arrival of her son. She, fearing that the report might reach the ears of the Emperor, ordered her son to be brought to her. When she saw him approaching, she went to meet him and handed him over to one of her confidants, whom she always intrusted with commissions of this kind. In what manner the unfortunate youth disappeared I cannot say. He has never been seen to this day, not even after his mother's death.

At that time the morals of women were almost without exception corrupt. They were faithless to their husbands with absolute licence, since the crime of adultery brought neither danger nor harm upon them. When convicted of the offence, they escaped punishment, thanks to the Empress, to whom they immediately applied. Then, getting the verdict quashed on the ground that the charges were not proved, they in turn accused their husbands, who, although not convicted, were condemned to refund twice the amount of the dower, and, for the most part, were flogged and led away to prison, where they were permitted to look upon their adulterous wives again, decked out in fine garments and in the act of committing adultery without the slightest shame with their lovers, many of whom, by way of recompense, received offices and rewards. This was the reason why most husbands afterwards put up with unholy outrages on the part of their wives, and gladly endured them in silence in order to escape the lash. They even afforded them every opportunity to avoid being surprised.

Theodora claimed complete control of the State at her sole discretion. She appointed magistrates and ecclesiastical dignitaries. Her only care and anxiety was, and as to this she made the most careful investigation, to prevent any office being given to a good and honourable man, who might be prevented by his conscience from assisting her in her nefarious designs.

She ordered all marriages as it were by a kind of divine authority; men never made a voluntary agreement before marriage. A wife was found for each without any previous notice, not because she pleased him (as is generally the case even amongst the barbarians) but because Theodora so desired it. Brides also had to put up with the same treatment, and were obliged to marry husbands whom they did not desire. She often turned the bride out of bed herself, and, without any reason, dismissed the bridegroom before the marriage had been consummated, merely saying, in great anger, that she disapproved of her. Amongst others whom she treated in this manner was Leontius the "referendary," and Saturninus, the son of Hermogenes the late Master of Offices, whom she deprived of their wives. This Saturninus had a young maiden cousin of an age to marry, free-born and modest, whom Cyrillus, her father, had betrothed to him after the death of Hermogenes. After the bridal chamber had been made ready and everything prepared, Theodora imprisoned the youthful bridegroom, who was afterwards conducted to another chamber, and forced, in spite of his violent lamentations and tears, to wed the daughter of Chrysomallo. This Chrysomallo had formerly been a dancer and a common prostitute, and at that time lived with another woman like her, and with Indaro, in the palace, where, instead of devoting themselves to phallic worship and theatrical amusements, they occupied themselves with affairs of State together with Theodora.

Saturninus, having lain with his new wife and discovered that she had already lost her maidenhead, informed one of his friends that his wife was no virgin. When this reached the ears of Theodora, she ordered the servants to hoist him up, like a boy at school, upbraiding him with having behaved too saucily and having taken an unbecoming oath. She then had him severely flogged on the bare back, and advised him to restrain his talkative tongue for the future.

In my former writings I have already related her treatment of John of Cappadocia, which was due to a desire to avenge personal injuries, not to punish him for offences against the State, as is proved by the fact that she did nothing of the kind in the case of those who committed far greater cruelties against their subjects. The real cause of her hatred was, that he ventured to oppose her designs and accused her to the Emperor, so that they nearly came to open hostilities. I mention this here because, as I have already stated, in this work I am bound to state the real causes of events. When, after having inflicted upon him the sufferings I have related, she had confined him in Egypt, she was not even then satisfied with his punishment, but was incessantly on the look out to find false witnesses against him. Four years afterwards, she succeeded in finding two of the Green faction who had taken part in the sedition at Cyzicus, and were accused of having been accessory to the assault upon the Bishop. These she attacked with flattery, promises, and threats. One of them, alarmed and inveigled by her promises, accused John of the foul crime of murder, but the other refused to utter falsehoods, although he was so cruelly tortured that he seemed likely to die on the spot. She was, therefore, unable to compass the death of John on this pretext, but she caused the young men's right hands to be chopped off, that of the one because he refused to bear false witness; that of the other, to prevent her intrigue becoming universally known, for she endeavoured to keep secret from others those things which were done in the open market-place.

CHAPTER XVIII

That Justinian was not a man, but a demon in human shape, as I have already said, may be abundantly proved by considering the enormity of the evils which he inflicted upon mankind, for the power of the acting cause is manifested in the excessive atrocity of his actions. I think that God alone could accurately reckon the number of those who were destroyed by him, and it would be easier for a man to count the grains of sand on the sea-shore than the number of his victims. Considering generally the extent of country which was depopulated by him, I assert that more than two millions of people perished. He so devastated the vast tract of Libya that a traveller, during a long journey, considered it a remarkable thing to meet a single man; and yet there were eighty thousand Vandals who bore arms, besides women, children and servants without number. In addition to these, who amongst men could enumerate the ancient inhabitants who dwelt in the cities, tilled the land, and traded on the coast, of whom I myself have seen vast numbers with my own eyes? The natives of Mauretania were even still more numerous, and they were all exterminated, together with their wives and children. This country also proved the tomb of numbers of Roman soldiers and of their auxiliaries from Byzantium. Therefore, if one were to assert that five millions perished in that country, I do not feel sure that he would not under-estimate the number. The reason of this was that Justinian, immediately after the defeat of the Vandals, did not take measures to strengthen his hold upon the country, and showed no anxiety to protect his interests by securing the goodwill of his subjects, but immediately recalled Belisarius on a charge of aspiring to royal power (which would by no means have suited him) in order that he might manage the affairs of the country at his own discretion, and ravage and plunder the whole of Libya. He sent commissioners to value the province, and imposed new and most harsh taxes upon the inhabitants. He seized the best and most fertile estates, and prohibited the Arians from exercising the rites of their religion. He was dilatory in keeping his army well supplied and in an effective condition, while in other respects he was a severe martinet, so that disturbances arose which ended in great loss. He was unable to abide by what was established, but was by nature prone to throw everything into a state of confusion and disturbance.

Italy, which was three times larger than Libya, was depopulated far more than the latter throughout its whole extent, whence a computation may be made of the number of those who perished there, for I have already spoken of the origin of the events that took place in Italy. All his crimes in Africa were repeated in Italy; having despatched Logothetae to this country also, he immediately overthrew and ruined everything.

Before the Italian war, the Empire of the Goths extended from the territory of the Gauls to the boundaries of Dacia, and the city of Sirmium; but, when the Roman army arrived in Italy, the greater part of Cisalpine Gaul and of the territory of the Venetians was in the occupation of the Germans. Sirmium and the adjacent country was in the hands of the Gepidae. The entire tract of country, however, was utterly depopulated; war and its attendant evils, disease and famine, had exterminated the inhabitants. Illyria and the whole of Thrace, that is to say, the countries between the Ionian Gulf and the suburbs of Byzantium, including Hellas and the Chersonese, were overrun nearly every year after the accession of Justinian by the Huns, Slavs and Antes, who inflicted intolerable sufferings upon the inhabitants. I believe that, on the occasion of each of these inroads, more than two hundred thousand Romans were either slain or carried away into slavery, so that the solitude of Scythia overspread these provinces.

Such were the results of the wars in Libya and Europe. During all this time, the Saracens also made perpetual inroads upon the Eastern Romans, from Egypt to the Persian frontiers, and harassed them so persistently, that those districts gradually became depopulated. I believe it would be impossible for anyone to estimate correctly the number of men who perished there.

The Persians under Chosroes thrice invaded the rest of the Roman territory, destroyed the cities, slew or carried off those whom they found in the captured towns in each district, and depopulated the country wherever they attacked it. From the time they entered Colchis, the losses were divided between themselves, the Lazes, and the Romans, as up to the present day.

However, neither Persians, Saracens, Huns, Slavs, nor any other barbarians were themselves able to evacuate Roman territory without considerable loss, for, in their inroads, and still more in their sieges and engagements, they often met with numerous reverses which inflicted equal disasters upon them. Thus not only the Romans, but almost all the barbarians, felt the bloodthirstiness of Justinian. Chosroes (as I have stated in the proper place) was certainly a man of depraved character, but it was Justinian who always took the initiative in bringing about war with this prince, for he took no care to adapt his policy to circumstances, but did everything at the wrong moment. In time of peace or truce, his thoughts were ever craftily engaged in endeavouring to find pretexts for war against his neighbours. In war, he lost heart without reason, and, owing to his meanness, he never made his preparations in good time; and, instead of devoting his earnest attention to such matters, he busied himself with the investigation of heavenly phenomena and with curious researches into the nature of God. Nevertheless, he would not abandon war, being by nature tyrannical and bloodthirsty, although he was unable to overcome his enemies, since his meanness prevented him from making the necessary preparations. Thus, during the reign of this prince, the whole world was deluged with the blood of nearly all the Romans and barbarians.

Such were the events that took place, during the wars abroad, throughout the whole of the Roman Empire; but the disturbances in Byzantium and every other city caused equal bloodshed; for, since no regard was had to justice or impartiality in meting out punishment for offences, each faction being eager to gain the favour of the Emperor, neither party was able to keep quiet. They alternately abandoned themselves to the madness of despair or presumptuous vanity, according as they failed or succeeded in ingratiating themselves with him. Sometimes they attacked one another en masse, sometimes in small bands, sometimes in single combat, or set ambuscades for each other at every opportunity. For thirty-two years without intermission they inflicted horrible cruelties upon one another. They were frequently put to death by the Praefect of the city, although punishment for offences fell most heavily upon the Green faction. The punishment of the Samaritans also, and other so-called heretics, deluged the Roman Empire with blood. Let it suffice, on the present occasion, to recall briefly what I have already narrated in greater detail. These calamities, which afflicted the whole world, took place during the reign of this demon in the form of a man, for which he himself, when Emperor, was responsible. I will now proceed to relate the evils he wrought by some hidden force and demoniacal power.

During his control of the Empire, numerous disasters of various kinds occurred, which some attributed to the presence and artifices of his evil genius, while others declared that the Divinity, in detestation of his works, having turned away in disgust from the Roman Empire, had given permission to the avenging deities to inflict these misfortunes. The river Scirtus overflowed Edessa, and brought the most grievous calamities upon the inhabitants of the district, as I have already related. The Nile, having overflown its banks as usual, did not subside at the ordinary time, and caused great suffering among the people. The Cydnus was swollen, and nearly the whole of Tarsus lay for several days under water; and it did not subside until it had wrought irreparable damage to the city.

Several cities were destroyed by earth-quake, Antioch, the chief city of the East, Seleucia, and Anazarbus, the most famous town in Cilicia. Who could calculate the numbers of those who were thereby destroyed? To these cities we may add Ibora, Amasea (the chief city of Pontus), Polybotus in Phrygia (called Polymede by the Pisidians), Lychnidus in Epirus, and Corinth, cities which from ancient times had been thickly populated. All these cities were overthrown at that time by an earthquake, during which nearly all their inhabitants perished. Afterwards the plague (which I have spoken of before) began to rage, and swept away nearly half the survivors. Such were the disasters that afflicted mankind, from the day when Justinian first commenced to manage the affairs of the kingdom to the time, and after he had ascended the Imperial throne.

CHAPTER XIX

I will now relate the manner in which he got possession of the wealth of the world, after I have first mentioned a vision which was seen in a dream by a person of distinction at the commencement of his reign. He thought he was standing on the coast at Byzantium, opposite Chalcedon, and saw Justinian standing in the midst of the channel. The latter drank up all the water of the sea, so that it seemed as if he were standing on dry land, since the water no longer filled the strait. After this, other streams of water, full of filth and rubbish, flowing in from the underground sewers on either side, covered the dry land. Justinian again swallowed these, and the bed of the channel again became dry. Such was the vision this person beheld in his dream.

This Justinian, when his uncle Justin succeeded to the throne, found the treasury well filled, for Anastasius, the most provident and economical of all the Emperors, fearing (what actually happened) that his successor, if he found himself in want of money, would probably plunder his subjects, filled the treasure-houses with vast stores of gold before his death. Justinian exhausted all this wealth in a very short time, partly by senseless buildings on the coast, partly by presents to the barbarians, although one would have imagined that a successor, however profligate and extravagant, would have been unable to have spent it in a hundred years; for the superintendents of the treasures and other royal possessions asserted that Anastasius, during his reign of more than twenty-seven years, had without any difficulty accumulated 320,000 centenars, of which absolutely nothing remained, it having all been spent by this man during the lifetime of his uncle, as I have related above. It is impossible to describe or estimate the vast sums which he appropriated to himself during his lifetime by illegal means and wasted in extravagance; for he swallowed up the fortunes of his subjects like an ever-flowing river, daily absorbing them in order to disgorge them amongst the barbarians. Having thus squandered the wealth of the State, he cast his eyes upon his private subjects. Most of them he immediately deprived of their possessions with unbounded rapacity and violence, at the same time bringing against the wealthy inhabitants of Byzantium, and those of other cities who were reputed to be so, charges utterly without foundation. Some were accused of polytheism, others of heresy; some of sodomy, others of amours with holy women; some of unlawful intercourse, others of attempts at sedition; some of favouring the Green faction, others of high treason, or any other charge that could be brought against them. On his own responsibility he made himself heir not only of the dead, but also of the living, as opportunity offered. In such matters he showed himself an accomplished diplomatist. I have already mentioned above how he profited by the sedition named Nika which was directed against him, and immediately made himself heir of all the members of the Senate, and how, shortly before the sedition broke out, he obtained possession of the fortunes of private individuals. On every occasion he bestowed handsome presents upon all the barbarians alike, those of East and West, and North and South, as far as the inhabitants of the British Islands and of the whole world, nations of whom we had not even heard before, and whose names we did not know, until we became acquainted with them through their ambassadors. When these nations found out Justinian's disposition, they flocked to Byzantium from all parts of the world to present themselves to him. He, without any hesitation, overjoyed at the occurrence, and regarding it as a great piece of good luck to be able to drain the Roman treasury and fling its wealth to barbarians or the waves of the sea, dismissed them every day loaded with handsome presents. In this manner the barbarians became absolute masters of the wealth of the Romans, either by the donations which they received from the Emperor, their pillaging of the Empire, the ransom of their prisoners, or their trafficking in truces. This was the signification of the dream which I have mentioned above.

CHAPTER XX

Besides this, Justinian found other means of contriving to plunder his subjects, not en masse and at once, but by degrees and individually. These methods I will now proceed to describe as well as I am able. First of all he appointed a new magistrate, who had the right of conferring upon all those who kept shops the privilege of selling their wares at whatever price they pleased, on payment of a yearly rent to the Emperor. The citizens were compelled to make their purchases in the market, where they paid three times as much as elsewhere; nor, although he suffered severe loss, was the purchaser allowed to claim damages from anyone, for part of the profit went to the Emperor, and part to increase the salary of these officials. Purchasers were equally cheated by the magistrates' servants, who took part in these disgraceful transactions, while the shopkeepers, who were allowed to put themselves beyond reach of the law, inflicted great hardships upon their customers, not merely by raising their prices many times over, but by being guilty of unheard-of frauds in regard to their wares. Afterwards, Justinian instituted several "monopolies," as they were called, and sold the liberty of the subject to any who were willing to undertake this disgraceful traffic, after having settled with them the price that was to be paid. This done, he allowed those with whom he had made the bargain to carry out the management of the affair in whatever way they thought fit. He made these disgraceful arrangements, without any attempt at concealment, with all the other magistrates, who plundered their subjects with less apprehension, either themselves or through their agents, since some part of the profits of the plunder always fell to the share of the Emperor. Under the pretence that the former magistrates were insufficient to carry out these arrangements (although the city prefect had previously been able to deal with all criminal charges) he created two new ones. His object in this was, that he might have at his disposal a larger number of informers, and that he might the more easily inflict punishment and torture upon the innocent. One of these was called Praetor of the People, whose nominal duty it was to deal with thieves; the second was called the Commissioner, whose function it was to punish all cases of paederasty, buggery, superstition and heresy. If the Praetor found any articles of value amongst stolen goods, he handed them over to the Emperor, declaring that no owner could be found for them, and in this manner Justinian every day got possession of something of very great value. The Commissioner, after he had condemned offenders, confiscated what he pleased out of their estates and bestowed it upon the Emperor, who thus, in defiance of the law, enriched himself out of the fortunes of others; for the servants of these magistrates did not even take the trouble at the commencement of the trial to bring forward accusers or to produce any witnesses to the offences, but, during the whole of this period, without intermission, unexamined and unconvicted, the accused were secretly punished by death and the confiscation of their property by the Emperor.

Afterwards, this accursed wretch ordered both these magistrates and the city prefect to deal with all criminal affairs indifferently, bidding them enter into rivalry to see which of them could destroy the greatest number of citizens in the shortest time. It is said that, when one of them asked him which of them should have the decision if anyone was accused before all three, he replied, "Whichever of you has anticipated the others."

He debased the office of Quaestor, which almost all the preceding Emperors had held in especial regard, so that it was only filled by men of wisdom and experience, who above all were learned in the law and free from all suspicion of corruptibility, for it was felt that it would unavoidably be disastrous to the State if it were to be filled by men without experience or who were the slaves of avarice. This Emperor first bestowed it upon Tribonianus, whose character and misdeeds I have sufficiently described elsewhere. After his death, Justinian seized part of his estate, although he had left a son and several relatives who survived him. He then appointed Junilus (a Libyan by birth), a man who had not so much as a hearsay knowledge of law, for he had not even studied it in the public schools. Although he had a knowledge of Latin, he had never had any tuition in Greek, and was unable to speak the language. Frequently, when he attempted to say a few words in Greek, he was laughed at by his own servants. He was so mad after filthy lucre, that he had not the least scruple in publicly selling letters of office signed by the Emperor, and was never ashamed to stretch out his hand to those who had to do with him for a stater of gold. For no less than seven years the State dured the shame and ridicule brought upon it by this officer.

On the death of Junilus, Justinian elevated to this office Constantine, who was not unacquainted with law, but was very young and had never yet taken part in a trial; besides which, he was the most abandoned thief and braggart in the world. Justinian entertained the highest regard for him and showed him very great favour, condescending to make him the chief instrument of his extortion and sole arbiter in legal decisions. By this means Constantine in a short time amassed great wealth, but his insolence was outrageous, and his pride led him to treat everyone with contempt. Even those who were desirous of making him considerable presents were obliged to intrust them to those who seemed to be most in his confidence, for no one was permitted to approach or converse with him, except when he was hurrying to or returning from the Emperor. Even then he did not slacken his pace, but walked on hastily, for fear that those who approached him might waste his time without paying for it. Such was the manner in which Justinian dealt with the Quaestorship.

CHAPTER XXI

The Praefect of the supreme tribunals, besides the public tax, annually paid to the Emperor more than thirty centenars of gold. This sum was called the "aerial tribute," doubtless because it was no regular or usual one, but seemed to have fallen as it were by chance from Heaven, whereas it ought rather to have been called "the impost of his wickedness," for it served as a pretext to those functionaries, who were invested with high power, to plunder their subjects incessantly without fear of punishment. They pretended that they had to hand over the tribute to the Emperor, and they themselves, without any difficulty, acquired sufficient sums to secure regal affluence for themselves. Justinian allowed them to go on unchecked and unheeded, waiting until they had amassed great wealth, when it was his practice to bring against them some charge from which they could not readily clear themselves, and to confiscate the whole of their property, as he had treated John of Cappadocia. All those who held this office during his reign became wealthy to an extraordinary degree, and suddenly, with two exceptions. One of these was Phocas, of whom I have spoken in my previous writings, a man in the highest degree observant of integrity and honesty; who, during his tenure of office, was free from all suspicion of illegal gain. The other was Bassus, who was appointed later. Neither of them enjoyed their dignity for a year. At the end of a few months they were deprived of it as being incapable and unsuited to the times. But, not to go into details in every case, which would be endless, I will merely say that it was the same with all the other magistrates of Byzantium.

In all the cities throughout the Empire, Justinian selected for the highest offices the most abandoned persons he could find, and sold to them for vast sums the positions which they degraded. In fact, no honest man, possessed of the least common sense, would ever have thought of risking his own fortune in order to plunder those who had committed no offence. When Justinian had received the money from those with whom he made the bargain, he gave them full authority to deal with their subjects as they pleased, so that, by the destruction of provinces and populations, they might enrich themselves in the future; for, since they had borrowed large sums from the bankers at heavy rates of interest to purchase their magistracies, and had paid the sum due to him who sold them, when they arrived in the cities, they treated their subjects with every kind of tyranny, paying heed to nothing save how they might fulfil their engagements with their creditors and lay up great wealth for themselves. They had no apprehension that their conduct would bring upon them the risk of punishment; on the contrary, they expected that the greater number of those whom they plundered put to death without cause, the greater the reputation they would attain, for the name of murderer and robber was regarded as a proof of activity. But when Justinian learned that they had amassed considerable wealth during office, he entangled them in his net, and on some pretence or other deprived them of all their riches in a moment.

He had published an edict that candidates for offices should swear that they would keep themselves free from extortion, that they would neither give nor receive anything for their offices, and uttered against those who transgressed the law the most violent curses of ancient times. The law had not been in force a year when, forgetting its terms and the malediction which had been pronounced, he shamelessly put up these offices for sale, not secretly, but publicly in the market-place, and those who purchased them, in spite of their oaths to the contrary plundered and ravaged with greater audacity than before.

He afterwards thought of another contrivance, which may seem incredible. He resolved no longer to put up for sale, as before, the offices which he believed to be of greatest repute in Byzantium and other cities, but sought out a number of hired persons, whom he appointed at a fixed salary, and ordered to bring all the revenues to himself. These men, having received their salary, shamelessly got together from every country and carried off everything that they could. The stipendiary commission went from one place to another, plundering the subjects of the Empire in the name of their office.

Thus the Emperor exercised in every case the greatest care in the selection of these agents of his, who were truly the greatest scoundrels in the world; nor were his efforts and industry in this detestable business unsuccessful. When he advanced the first of his wicked agents to high offices, and the licence of authority revealed their corruption, we were astounded to think how the nature of man could be capable of such enormity. But when those who succeeded them far outdid them, men were at a loss to understand how their predecessors could have appeared the most wicked of mankind, since, in comparison with their successors, who had surpassed them in evil-doing, they might be considered good and honest men. But the third set and their successors so far outstripped the second in every kind of villainy, and in their cleverness in inventing new accusations, that they secured for their predecessors a certain reputation and a good name. As the misfortunes of the State increased, all learned by experience that there is no limit to the innate wickedness of man, and that, when it is supported by the knowledge of precedents, and encouraged by the power in its hands to torment its victims, no man can tell how far it will extend, but only the thoughts of the oppressed are capable of estimating it. Such was the state of affairs in regard to the magistrates.

The hostile armies of the Huns had often reduced to slavery and plundered the inhabitants of the Empire. The Thracian and Illyrian generals resolved to attack them on their retreat, but turned back when they were shown letters from the Emperor forbidding them to attack the barbarians, on pretence that their help was necessary to the Romans against the Goths and other enemies of the Empire.

Making use of this opportunity, these barbarians plundered the country like enemies, and carried away the inhabitants into slavery; and in this manner these pretended friends and allies of the Romans returned home with their plunder and a number of prisoners. Frequently, some of the peasants in those parts, urged on by a longing for their wives and children who had been carried away into slavery, formed themselves into bands, marched against the barbarians, slew a number of them, and succeeded in capturing their horses together with their plunder. This success, however, proved very unfortunate for them; for agents were sent from Byzantium, who had no hesitation in beating and wounding them and seizing their property, until they had restored all the horses that they had taken from the barbarians.

CHAPTER XXII

After the Emperor and Empress had destroyed John of Cappadocia, they were desirous of appointing someone else to his office, and agreed to search for a man even more vicious than he. They looked around to find this instrument of tyranny, and examined the dispositions of all, in order that they might the more speedily be able to ruin their subjects. They temporarily conferred the office upon Theodotus, who, though certainly not an honourable man, was not sufficiently wicked to satisfy them. They continued their search in all directions, and at last by accident found a banker named Peter, a Syrian by birth, surnamed Barsyames. He had long sat at the copper money-changer's counter, and had amassed large sums by his disgraceful malpractices. He was exceedingly cunning at thieving obols, ever deceiving his customers by the quickness of his fingers. He was very clever at filching without ado what fell into his hands, and, when detected, he swore that it was the fault of his hands, and made use of most impudent language in order to conceal his guilt.

This Barsyames, having been enrolled in the praetorian guard, behaved so outrageously that he approved himself beyond all others to Theodora, and was selected by her to assist in carrying out those of her nefarious schemes which required the most inventive genius. For this reason Justinian and Theodora immediately deprived Theodotus of the dignity bestowed upon him as the successor of the Cappadocian, and appointed Peter in his stead, who in every respect acted in accordance with their wishes.

He not only, without the least fear or shame, cheated the soldiers of their pay, but offered commands and offices for sale to a greater extent than before. Having thus degraded them, he sold them to persons who were not ashamed to engage in this unholy traffic, giving express permission to the purchasers to deal as they pleased with the lives and properties of those who were subject to their authority; for Barsyames claimed for himself and granted to anyone who had paid down the price of a province the right of plundering and ravaging it at pleasure. It was from the chief of the State that this traffic in lives proceeded, and agreements were entered into for the ruin of the cities. In the chief courts and in the public market-place the legalised brigand went round about, who was called "collector" from his duty of collecting the money paid for the purchase of dignities, which they exacted from the oppressed, who had no hope of redress. Of all those who were promoted to his service, although several were men of repute, Barsyames always preferred such as were of depraved character.

He was not the only offender in this respect; all his predecessors and successors were equally guilty. The "Master of Offices" did the same, likewise the officials of the imperial treasury, and those who had the duty of superintending the Emperor's private and personal estate, in a word, all who held public appointments in Byzantium and other cities. In fact, from the time that this tyrant had the management of affairs, either he or his minister claimed the subsidies suitable to each office, and those who served their superiors, suffering extreme poverty, were compelled to submit to be treated as if they were the most worthless slaves.

The greater part of the corn that had been imported to Byzantium was kept until it rotted; but, although it was not fit for human consumption, he forced the cities of the East to purchase it in proportion to their importance, and he demanded payment, not at the price paid even for the best corn, but at a far higher rate; and the poor people, who had been forced to purchase it at an outrageously heavy price, were compelled to throw it into the sea or the drains.

That which was sound and not yet spoilt, of which there was great abundance in the capital, the Emperor determined to sell to those cities which were scantily supplied. In this manner he realised twice the amount that had formerly been obtained by the receivers of the public tribute in the provinces. The next year the supply of corn was not so abundant, and the transports did not bring a sufficient quantity to supply the needs of the capital. Peter, disconcerted at the state of affairs, conceived the idea of buying up a great quantity of corn from Bithynia, Phrygia and Thrace. The inhabitants of those provinces were forced to bring it down to the coasts themselves (a work of great labour), and to convey it at considerable risk to Byzantium, where they had to be satisfied with an absurdly low price. Their losses were so considerable, that they would have preferred to have given the corn gratuitously to the public granaries, and even to have paid twice as much. This burdensome duty was called Syn=on=e, or provisioning the capital with corn from the provinces. But, as even then the supply of corn was not sufficient for the needs of the city, many complaints were made to the Emperor. At the same time the soldiers, hardly any of whom had as yet received their pay, assembled and created a great disturbance in the city. The Emperor appeared greatly irritated against Peter, and resolved to deprive him of his office, both for the reasons stated and also because it was reported to him that he had amassed extraordinary wealth, which he kept hidden away, by robbing the public treasury; and this in fact was the case. But Theodora opposed her husband's intention, being exceedingly enamoured of Barsyames, apparently on account of his evil character and the remarkable cruelty with which he treated his subjects; for, being herself exceedingly cruel and utterly inhuman, she was anxious that the character of her agents should be in conformity with her own. It is also said that Theodora, against her will, had been forced by the enchantments of Barsyames to become his friend; for this man had devoted great attention to sorcerers and supernatural beings, admired the Manichaeans, and was not ashamed openly to profess himself their supporter. Although the Empress was not ignorant of this, she did not withdraw her favour, but resolved on this account to show even greater interest and regard for him than before, for she herself also, from her earliest years, had associated with sorcerers and magicians, since her character and pursuits inclined her towards them. She had great faith in their arts, and placed the greatest confidence in them. It is even said that she did not render Justinian susceptible to her influence so much by her flatteries as by the irresistible power of evil spirits; for Justinian was not sufficiently kindly, or just, or persistent in well-doing to be superior to such secret influence, but was manifestly dominated by a thirst for blood and riches, and fell an easy prey to those who deceived and flattered him. In undertakings which needed the greatest attention, he changed his plans without any reason and showed himself as light as the dust swept before the wind. Thus none of his kinsmen or friends had the least confidence in his stability, but, in the execution of his purpose, his opinion perpetually changed with the greatest rapidity. Being, as I have said, an easy object of attack for the sorcerers, he in like manner readily fell a victim to Theodora, who, for this reason, entertained the highest affection for Peter as one devoted to the study of these arts.

The Emperor only succeeded with great difficulty in depriving him of his office, and, at the pressing entreaty of Theodora, soon afterwards appointed him chief of the treasury, and deprived John of these functions, although he had only been invested with them a few months previously. This John was a native of Palestine, a good and gentle man, who did not even know how to find out the means of increasing his private fortune, and had never done injury to a single individual. The more decided the affection of the people for him, the less he met with the approval of Justinian and his partner, who, as soon as they found amongst their agents, contrary to expectation, a good and honourable man, were quite dumbfounded, showed their indignation, and endeavoured by every possible means to get rid of him with the least delay. Thus Peter succeeded John as chief of the royal treasury, and was one of the chief causes of great misery to all the inhabitants of the Empire. He embezzled the greater part of the fund, which, in accordance with an ancient custom, was annually distributed by the Emperor to a number of families by way of assisting them. Part of this public money he sent to the Emperor, and kept part for himself, whereby he acquired ill-gotten wealth. Those who were thus deprived of this money lived in a pitiable state. He did not even coin the same amount of gold as before, but less, a thing which had never been done before. Such was the manner in which Justinian dealt with the magistracies.

CHAPTER XXIII

I will now relate how he everywhere ruined the possessors of estates, although, to show their misery, it would really be sufficient to refer to what has been said, just before this, concerning the governors dispatched to all the provinces and cities, for it was they who plundered those who possessed landed estates, as before related.

It had long been an established custom that the Roman Emperor should, not only once, but on several occasions, remit to his subjects all the arrears that were owing to the treasury, so that those who were in difficulties and had no means of settling these arrears might not be continually pressed, and that the tax collectors might not have an excuse for vexatiously attempting to exact money from those liable to tribute, where in many cases it was not due. Justinian, however, for thirty-two years made no concession of the kind to his subjects, the result of which was that the poor people were forced to quit the country without any hope of return. The more honest were perpetually harassed by these false accusers, who threatened to charge them with having paid less than the amount at which they were rated. These unhappy individuals were less afraid of the imposition of new taxes than of the insupportable weight of the unjust exactions which for many years they had been compelled to pay, whereupon many of them abandoned their property to their accusers or to the rise.

The Medes and Saracens had ravaged the greater part of Asia, and the Huns and Slavs had plundered the whole of Europe. Cities had been razed to the ground or subjected to severe exactions; the inhabitants had been carried away into slavery with all they possessed, and every district had been deserted by its inhabitants in consequence of the daily inroads. Justinian, however, remitted no tax or impost to any one of them, except in the case of cities that had been taken by the enemy, and then only for a year, although, had he granted them exemption for seven years, as the Emperor Anastasius had done, I do not think that even then he would have done enough: for Cabades retired after having inflicted but little damage upon the buildings, but Chosroes, by ravaging the country with fire and sword and razing all its dwellings to the ground, brought greater calamities upon the inhabitants. Justinian only granted this absurd remission of tribute to these people and to others who had several times submitted to an invasion of the Medes and the continuous depredations of the Huns and Saracen barbarians in the East, while the Romans, settled in the different parts of Europe, who had equally suffered by the attacks of the barbarians, found Justinian more cruel than any of their foreign foes; for, immediately after the enemy withdrew, the proprietors of estates found themselves overwhelmed with requisitions for provisions,[13] impositions,[14] and edicts[15] of various kinds, the meaning of which I will now explain. Those who possessed landed property were obliged to furnish provisions for the soldiers in proportion to the amount imposed upon each, and these dues were fixed, not in consideration of the necessities of the moment, but according to an authorised imperial assessment; and, if at any time they had not a sufficient supply upon their lands for the needs of the horses and soldiers, these unhappy persons were forced to purchase them even at a price far above their proper value, and to convey them in many cases from a considerable distance to the place where the troops were encamped, and to distribute them to the adjutants in what quantity and at what rate the latter pleased, not at a fair and reasonable price. This import was called "the import of victualling," which, as it were, cut the sinews of all the landed proprietors; for they had to pay an annual tribute ten times greater than before, and were obliged not only to furnish supplies the soldiers, but on several occasions to convey corn to Byzantium. Barsyames was not the only man who had the audacity to introduce this cursed exaction, John of Cappadocia had set the example, and the successors of Barsyames in his office followed it. Such was the nature of the Syn[=o]n[=e], as it was called.

The "Epibol[=e]" was a kind of unforeseen ruin, which suddenly attacked the landed proprietors and utterly deprived them of the hope of subsistence; for, in the case of estates that were deserted and unproductive, the owners or tenants of which had either died or abandoned their country and hidden themselves after the misfortunes they had undergone, Justinian did not hesitate to impose a tax. Such were these "impositions," which were of frequent occurrence during that time.

A few words will suffice for the impost called "Diagraph[=e]." At this time especially, the cities were afflicted with heavy losses, the causes and extent of which I will say nothing about, for it would be an endless tale. These losses had to be repaired by the landed proprietors in proportion to the rate at which they were assessed. Their misery, however, did not stop there, but, although pestilence had attacked the whole world, and, especially, the Roman Empire; although most of the farmers had fallen victims, and their properties had become deserted, Justinian did not show the least clemency towards the owners. He continued to exact the yearly tribute from them, not only their own proportion, but that of their neighbours who had died of the plague.[16] Further, they were obliged to treat the soldiers with the greatest civility, and to allow them to take up their quarters in their finest and richest apartments, while they themselves all the time had to content themselves with the poorest and meanest rooms. Such were the calamities that without intermission befell mankind during the reign of Justinian and Theodora, for there was no cessation of war or any other most terrible calamities. Since I have mentioned the word "quarters," I must not forget to say that at one time there were 70,000 barbarians at Constantinople, whom house owners were obliged to quarter, being thus shut out from all enjoyment of their own, and in many other ways inconvenienced.

CHAPTER XXIV

I must not, however, omit to mention the manner in which Justinian treated the soldiers. He appointed commissioners, called Logothetae,[17] with directions to squeeze as much money as they could out of them, a twelfth part of the sum thus obtained being assured to them. The following was their mode of operation every year. It was an established custom that the soldiers should not all have the same pay. Those who were young, and had just joined, received less than those who had undergone hardships in the field and were already half-way up the list; while the veterans, whose term of service was all but over, received a more considerable sum, that they might have sufficient to live upon as private individuals, and, after their death, might be able to leave a small inheritance by way of consolation to their families. Thus, in course of time, the soldiers gradually rose in rank, according as their comrades died or retired from the service, and their pay from the public funds was regulated in accordance with their seniority. But these commissioners would not allow the names of those who had died or fallen in battle to be struck out, or the vacancies to be filled, until a long interval had elapsed. The result was, that the army was short of men, and the survivors, after the death of the veterans, were kept in a position far inferior to their merits, and received less pay than they ought to have done, while in the meantime the commissioners handed over to Justinian the money they thus purloined from the soldiers. In addition, they harassed the soldiers with several other kinds of injustices, by way of recompense for the dangers they had undergone in the field; they were taunted with the name of Greeks, as if Greece could never produce a brave soldier; others were cashiered, as not having been ordered by the Emperor to serve, although they showed their commissions, the genuineness of which the Logothetae did not hesitate to call in question; others, again, were disbanded for having absented themselves a short time from their quarters. Afterwards, some of the Palace Guards were sent into every part of the Empire to take an exact inventory of the soldiers who were or were not fit for service. Some were deprived of their belts, as being useless and too old, and for the future were obliged to solicit alms from the charitable in the open market-place, a sad and melancholy spectacle to all beholders. The rest were reduced to such a state of terror that, in order to avoid similar treatment, they offered large sums of money to buy themselves out, so that the soldiers, being thus rendered destitute and in many ways enfeebled, conceived an utter aversion to the service.

This endangered the authority of the Romans, especially in Italy. Alexander, who was sent thither as commissioner, unhesitatingly reproached the soldiers for this. He also exacted large sums of money from the Italians, under the pretence of punishing them for their negotiations with Theoderic and the Goths. The soldiers were not the only persons who were reduced to poverty and privation by the commissioners; but those who had accompanied the generals in different capacities and had formerly enjoyed a high reputation, found themselves in great distress, as they had no means of procuring the ordinary necessaries. Since I am speaking of the soldiers, I will give a few additional details. Preceding Emperors had, for a very long time past, carefully posted upon all the frontiers of the Empire a large military force to protect its boundaries, and particularly, in the Eastern provinces, in order to repel the inroads of the Persians and Saracens, they had established garrisons called "frontier troops." Justinian at first treated these troops with such shameful neglect that their pay was four, or even five years in arrear; and, when peace was concluded between Rome and Persia, these unhappy individuals, who expected to enjoy the advantages of peace, were obliged to make a present to the treasury of the money due to them; and the Emperor finally disbanded them most unjustly. Thus the frontiers of the Roman Empire remained ungarrisoned, and the troops had nothing to subsist upon except the benevolence of the charitable.

There was a certain body of soldiers, about 3,500 in number, called "Scholares," who had been originally appointed as an imperial palace-guard, and received a larger pay from the imperial treasury than the rest of the army. They were first chosen according to merit from the Armenians; but, from the reign of Zeno, anyone, however cowardly and unwarlike, was allowed to enter this body. In course of time, even slaves, on payment of a sum of money, were admitted to their ranks. When Justin succeeded to the throne, Justinian enrolled a large number on payment of considerable sums of money. When the list was filled up, he added about 2,000 more who were called "Supernumeraries," but disbanded them, when he himself came to the throne, without any reimbursement. In regard to these "Scholares," he invented the following plan: Whenever it was probable that an expedition would be despatched to Italy, Libya, or Persia, he ordered them to make ready to take part in the campaign, although he knew that they were utterly unfit for war; and they, being afraid of this, surrendered their salaries to the Emperor. This was a frequent occurrence. When Peter was "Master of Offices," he daily harassed them with monstrous thefts. This man, although he was of a mild and by no means overbearing disposition, was the greatest thief in the world and an absolute slave to sordid avarice. He it was who (as I have related) contrived the murder of Amalasunta, the daughter of Theodoric.

There are in the imperial household other officers of much higher rank, who, having purchased their positions for a larger sum, receive better pay in proportion. These are called "Domestics" and "Protectors." They have always been exempt from military service, and are only reckoned members of the palace on account of their dignity and rank. Some of them are constantly in Byzantium, while others have long been established in Galatia or other provinces. Justinian frightened these in the same manner into abandoning their salaries to him. In conclusion, it was the custom that, every five years, the Emperor should present each of the soldiers with a fixed sum in gold. Accordingly, every five years, commissioners were despatched to all parts of the Empire, to bestow five staters of gold upon every soldier as a gift from the Emperor. This had long been an established and inviolable practice. But, from the day that Justinian assumed the management of affairs, he did nothing of the kind, and showed no intention of doing so during the thirty-two years of his reign, so that the custom was almost completely forgotten.

CHAPTER XXV

I will now proceed to mention another mode in which he plundered his subjects. Those who, at Byzantium, serve the Emperor or magistrates, either as secretaries, or in a military or any other capacity, are placed last upon the list of officials. As time goes on, they are gradually promoted to the place of those who have died or retired, until they reach the highest rank and supreme dignity. Those who had attained to this honour, in accordance with an ancient institution, had the right to the enjoyment of a fund of not less than 100 centenars of gold yearly, so that they might have a comfortable means of subsistence for their old age, and might be able to assist others as much as possible; and this was of great influence in bringing about a successful administration of the affairs of state. But Justinian deprived them of all their privileges, and did great harm, not only to them, but to many others besides, for the poverty which attacked them extended to all those who formerly shared their prosperity. If anyone were to calculate the sums of which they were thus deprived during these thirty-two years, he would find that the amount was very considerable. Such was the shameful manner in which the tyrant treated his soldiers.

I will now relate how he behaved towards merchants, mariners, artisans, shopkeepers and others. There are two narrow straits on either side of Byzantium, the one in the Hellespont, between Sestos and Abydos, the other at the mouth of the Euxine Sea, close to the chapel of the Holy Mother. In the strait upon the Hellespont, there was no public custom-house, but an officer was sent by the Emperor to Abydos, to see that no ship loaded with arms should pass on the way to Byzantium without the Emperor's leave, and also that no person should put out to sea from Byzantium without letters of licence signed by the proper official, no ship being allowed to leave the city without the permission of the secretaries of the Master of Offices. The amount which the praetor exacted from the shipmasters under the name of toll was so insignificant that it was disregarded. A praetor was also sent to the other strait, who received his salary regularly from the Emperor, and whose duties were the same, to take care that no one transported to the barbarians on the Euxine any wares, the export of which to hostile countries was forbidden; but he was not allowed to exact any duties from these navigators. But, from the day that Justinian succeeded to the government of affairs, he established a custom-house on both straits, and sent thither two officials to collect the dues at a fixed salary, who were ordered to get in as much money as they could. These officials, who desired nothing better than to show their devotion to him, extorted duty upon all kinds of merchandise. In regard to the port of Byzantium, he made the following arrangement: He put it in charge of one of his confidants, a Syrian by birth, named Addeus, whom he ordered to exact duty from all vessels which put in there. This Addeus would not allow those ships which had been any length of time in the harbour to leave it, until the masters had paid a sum of money to free them, or else he compelled them to take on board a freight for Libya or Italy. Some, resolved not to take in a return cargo or to remain at sea any longer, burned their ships and thus escaped all anxiety, to their great rejoicing. But all those who were obliged to continue their profession in order to live, for the future demanded three times the usual amount from merchants for the hire of the ships, and thus the merchants had no means of covering their losses except by requiring a higher price from purchasers; and thus, by every possible contrivance, the Romans were reduced to the danger of starvation. Such was the general state of affairs. I must not, however, omit to state the manner in which the rulers dealt with the small coinage. The money-changers had formerly been accustomed to give 210 obols (called Pholes) for a single gold stater. Justinian and Theodora, for their own private gain, ordered that only 180 obols should be given for the stater, and by this means deprived the public of a sixth part of each piece of gold. Having established "monopolies" upon most wares, they incessantly harassed would-be purchasers. The only thing left free from duty was clothes, but, in regard to these also, the imperial pair contrived to extort money. Silken garments had for a long time been made in Berytus and Tyre, cities of Phoenicia. The merchants and workmen connected with the trade had been settled there from very early times, and from thence the business had spread throughout the world. During the reign of Justinian, those who lived in Byzantium and other cities raised the price of their silks, on the plea that at the present time they were dearer in Persia, and that the import tithes were higher. The Emperor pretended to be exceedingly indignant at this, and subsequently published an edict forbidding a pound of silk to be sold for more than eight gold pieces; anyone who disobeyed the edict was to be punished by the confiscation of his property. This measure appeared altogether impracticable and absurd. For it was not possible for the merchants, who had bought their wares at a much higher price, to sell it to customers at a lower rate. They accordingly resolved to give up this business, and secretly and without delay disposed of their remaining wares to certain well-known persons, who took delight in wasting their money upon such adornments, and to whom it had become in a manner an absolute necessity. Theodora heard of this from certain persons who whispered it confidentially, and, without taking the trouble to verify the report, she immediately deprived these persons of their wares, and, in addition, inflicted upon them a fine of a centenar of gold. At the present time, the imperial treasurer is charged with the superintendence of this trade. When Peter Barsyames held the office, they soon allowed him all manner of licence in carrying out his nefarious practices. He demanded that all the rest should carefully observe the law, and compelled those who were engaged in the silk factories to work for himself alone. Without taking any trouble to conceal it, he sold an ounce of any ordinary coloured silk in the public market-place for six pieces of gold, but if it was of the royal dye, called Holovere, he asked more than four-and-twenty for it. In this manner he procured vast sums of money for the Emperor, and even larger sums, which he kept privately for himself; and this practice, begun by him, continued. The grand treasurer is at this moment avowedly the only silk merchant and sole controller of the market. All those who formerly carried on this business, either in Byzantium or any other city, workers on sea or land, felt the loss severely. Nearly the whole population of the cities which existed by such manufactories were reduced to begging. Artisans and mechanics were forced to struggle against hunger, and many of them, quitting their country, fled to Persia. None but the chief treasurer was allowed to have anything to do with that branch of industry, and, while he handed over part of his gains to the Emperor, he kept the greater part for himself, and thus grew wealthy at the expense of the unfortunate public.

CHAPTER XXVI

I must now relate how he robbed Byzantium and other cities of their ornaments. In the first place he resolved to humiliate the lawyers. He deprived them of all the fees, which, after they had finished their case, were considerable, and enriched them and increased their distinction. He ordered that litigants should come to an agreement upon oath, which brought the lawyers into contempt and insignificance. After he had seized the estates of the Senators and other families reputed wealthy, in Byzantium and throughout the Empire, the profession had little to do, for the citizens no longer possessed property worth disputing about. Thus, of the numerous and famous orators who once composed this order there remained only a few, who were everywhere despised and lived in the greatest poverty, finding that their profession brought them nothing but insult. He also caused physicians and professors of the liberal arts to be deprived of the necessaries of life. He cut off from them all the supplies which former emperors had attached to these professions, and which were paid out of the State funds. Further, he had no scruple about transferring to the public funds all the revenues which the inhabitants of the cities had devoted either to public purposes or for providing entertainments. From that time no attention was paid to physicians or professors; no one ventured to trouble himself about the public buildings; there were no public lights in the cities, or any enjoyments for the inhabitants; the performances in the theatres and hippodromes and the combats of wild beasts, in which Theodora had been bred and brought up, were entirely discontinued. He afterwards suppressed public exhibitions in Byzantium, to save the usual State contribution, to the ruin of an almost countless multitude who found their means of support in these entertainments. Their life, both in public and private, became sad and dejected and utterly joyless, as if some misfortune had fallen upon them from Heaven. Nothing was spoken of in conversation at home, in the streets, or in the churches, except misfortune and suffering. Such was the state of the cities.

I have still something important to mention. Every year two consuls were appointed, one at Rome, the other at Byzantium. Whoever was advanced to that dignity was expected to expend more than twenty centenars of gold upon the public. This sum was to a small extent furnished by the consuls themselves, while the greater part was due to the liberality of the Emperor. This money was distributed amongst those whom I have mentioned, above all to the most necessitous, and principally to those employed upon the stage, which materially increased the comfort of the citizens. But, since the accession of Justinian, the elections never took place at the proper time; sometimes one consul remained in office for several years, and at last people never even dreamed of a fresh appointment. This reduced all to the greatest distress; since the Emperor no longer granted the usual assistance to his subjects, and at the same time deprived them of what they had by every means in his power.

I think I have given a sufficient account of the manner in which this destroyer swallowed up the property of the members of the Senate and deprived them all of their substance, whether publicly or privately. I also think that I have said enough concerning the fraudulent accusations which he made use of, in order to get possession of the property of other families which were reputed to be wealthy. Lastly, I have described the wrongs he inflicted upon the soldiers and servants of those in authority and the militia in the palace; upon countrymen, the possessors and proprietors of estates, and professors of the arts and sciences; upon merchants, shipmasters and sailors; mechanics, artisans, and retail dealers; those who gained their livelihood by performing upon the stage; in a word, upon all who were affected by the misery of these. I must now speak of his treatment of the poor, the lower classes, the indigent, and the sick and infirm. I will then go on to speak of his treatment of the priests.

At first, as has been said, he got all the shops into his own hands, and having established monopolies of all the most necessary articles of life, exacted from his subjects more than three times their value. But if I were to enter into the details of all these monopolies, I should never finish my narrative, for they are innumerable.

He imposed a perpetual and most severe tax upon bread, which the artisans, the poor, and infirm were compelled to purchase. He demanded from this commodity a revenue of three centenars of gold every year, and those poor wretches were obliged to support themselves upon bread full of dust, for the Emperor did not blush to carry his avarice to this extent. Seizing upon this as an excuse, the superintendents of the markets, eager to fill their own pockets, in a short time acquired great wealth, and, in spite of the cheapness of food, reduced the poor to a state of artificial and unexpected famine; for they were not allowed to import corn from any other parts, but were obliged to eat bread purchased in the city.

One of the city aqueducts had broken, and a considerable portion of the water destined for the use of the inhabitants was lost. Justinian, however, took no notice of it, being unwilling to incur any expense for repairs, although a great crowd continually thronged round the fountains, and all the baths had been shut. Nevertheless, he expended vast sums without any reason or sense upon buildings on the seashore, and also built everywhere throughout the suburbs, as if the palaces, in which their predecessors had always been content to live, were no longer suitable for himself and Theodora; so that it was not merely parsimony, but a desire for the destruction of human life, that prevented him from repairing the aqueduct, for no one, from most ancient times, had ever shown himself more eager than Justinian to amass wealth, and at the same time to spend it in a most wasteful and extravagant manner. Thus this Emperor struck at the poorest and most miserable of his subjects through two most necessary articles of food, bread and water, by making the one difficult to procure, and the other too dear for them to buy.

It was not only the poor of Byzantium, however, that he harassed in this manner, but, as I will presently mention, the inhabitants of several other cities. When Theodoric had made himself master of Italy, in order to preserve some trace of the old constitution, he permitted the praetorian guards to remain in the palace and continued their daily allowance. These soldiers were very numerous.

There were the Silentiarii, the Domestici, and the Scholares, about whom there was nothing military except the name, and their salary was hardly sufficient to live upon. Theodoric also ordered that their children and descendants should have the reversion of this. To the poor, who lived near the church of Peter the Apostle, he distributed every year 3,000 bushels of corn out of the public stores. All continued to receive these donations until the arrival of Alexander Forficula[18] in Italy. He resolved to deprive them of it immediately; and, when the Emperor was informed of this, he approved of his conduct, and treated Alexander with still greater honour. During his journey, Alexander treated the Greeks in the following manner: The peasants of the district near the pass of Thermopylae had long manned the fortress, and, each in turn, mounted guard over the wall which blocks the pass, whenever there seemed any likelihood of an invasion of the barbarians. But Alexander, on his arrival, pretended that it was to the interest of the Peloponnesians not to leave the protection of the pass to the peasants. He established a garrison of about 2,000 soldiers, who were not paid out of the public funds, but by each of the cities in Greece. On this pretext, he transferred to the public treasury all the revenues of these towns which were intended for public purposes or to cover the expenses of shows and entertainments. He pretended that it was to be employed for the support of the soldiers, and in consequence, from that time, no public buildings or other objects of utility were erected or promoted either in Athens or throughout Greece. Justinian, however, hastened to give his sanction to all the acts of Forficula.

We must now speak of the poor of Alexandria. Amongst the lawyers of that city was one Hephaestus, who, having been appointed governor, suppressed popular disturbances by the terror he inspired, but at the same time reduced the citizens to the greatest distress. He immediately established a monopoly of all wares, which he forbade other merchants to sell. He reserved everything for himself alone, sold everything himself, and fixed the price by the capricious exercise of his authority. Consequently, the city was in the greatest distress from want of provisions; the poor no longer had a sufficient supply of what was formerly sold at a low rate, and especially felt the difficulty of obtaining bread; for the governor alone bought up all the corn that came from Egypt, and did not allow anyone else to purchase even so much as a bushel; and in this manner, he taxed the loaves and put upon them what price he pleased. By this means he amassed an enormous fortune, and was likewise careful to satisfy the greed of the Emperor. So great was the terror inspired by Hephaestus, that the people of Alexandria endured their ill-treatment in silence; and the Emperor, out of gratitude for the money which flowed into his exchequer from that quarter, conceived a great affection for Hephaestus. The latter, in order to secure in a still greater degree the favour of the Emperor, carried out the following plan. When Diocletian became Emperor of the Romans, he ordered a yearly distribution of corn to be made to the necessitous poor of Alexandria; and the people, settling its distribution amongst themselves, transmitted the right to their descendants. Hephaestus deprived the necessitous of 2,000,000 bushels yearly, and deposited it in the imperial granaries, declaring, in his despatch to the Emperor, that this grant of corn had previously been made in a manner that was neither just nor in conformity with the interests of the state. The Emperor approved of his conduct and became more attached to him than ever. The Alexandrians, whose hopes of existence depended upon this distribution, felt the cruelty bitterly, especially at the time of their distress.

CHAPTER XXVII

The evil deeds of Justinian were so numerous, that time would fail me if I were to attempt to relate them all. It will therefore be sufficient, if I select some of those which will exhibit his whole character to posterity, and which clearly show his dissimulation, his neglect of God, the priesthood, the laws, and the people which showed itself devoted to him. He was utterly without shame; he had no care for the interests or advantage of the state, and did not trouble himself about excusing his misdeeds, or, in fact, about anything else but how he might plunder and appropriate the wealth of the whole world.

To begin with, he appointed Paul bishop of Alexandria, at the time when Rhodon, a Phoenician by birth, was governor of the city. He ordered him to show the greatest deference to the bishop, and to execute all his instructions; for by this means he hoped to prevail upon the chief persons of the city to support the council of Chalcedon. There was also a certain Arsenius, a native of Palestine, who had made himself most necessary to the Empress, and, in consequence of her favour and the great wealth he had amassed, had attained the rank of a senator, although he was a man of most abandoned character. He belonged to the Samaritan sect, but, in order to preserve his authority, he assumed the name of Christian. His father and brother, who lived in Scythopolis, relying upon his authority and following his advice, bitterly persecuted the Christians in that city. Whereupon the citizens rose up against them, and put them to death most cruelly, which afterwards proved the cause of much misery to the inhabitants of Palestine. On that occasion neither Justinian nor the Empress inflicted any punishment upon Arsenius, although he was the principal cause of all those troubles. They contented themselves with forbidding him to appear at court, in order to satisfy the continued complaints that were preferred against him by the Christians.

This Arsenius, thinking to gratify the Emperor, set out with Paul to Alexandria to assist him generally, and, above all, to do his utmost to aid him in securing the favour of the inhabitants; for, during the time of his exclusion from the palace, he affirmed that he had made himself thoroughly acquainted with all the doctrines of Christianity. This displeased Theodora, who pretended to hold a different opinion to the Emperor in religious matters, as I have already stated.

When they arrived at Alexandria, Paul delivered over the deacon Psoes to the governor to be put to death, asserting that he was the only obstacle in the way of the realisation of the Emperor's desires. The governor, urged on by despatches from the Emperor, which frequently arrived and were couched in pressing terms, ordered Psoes to be flogged, and he died under the torture. When the news of this reached the Emperor, at the earnest entreaty of Theodora, he expressed great indignation against Paul, Rhodon, and Arsenius, as if he had forgotten the orders he himself had given them. He appointed Liberius, a Roman patrician, governor of Alexandria, and sent some priests of high repute to investigate the matter. Amongst them was Pelagius, archdeacon of Rome, who was commissioned by Pope Vigilius to act as his agent. Paul, being convicted of murder, was deprived of his bishopric; Rhodon, who had fled to Byzantium, was executed by order of Justinian, and his estate confiscated, although he produced thirteen despatches, in which the Emperor expressly ordered and insisted that he should in everything act in accordance with Paul's orders, and never oppose him, that he might have liberty to act as he pleased in matters of religion. Arsenius was crucified by Liberius, in accordance with instructions from Theodora; his estate was confiscated by the Emperor, although he had no cause of complaint against him except his intimacy with Paul. Whether in this he acted justly or not, I cannot say; but I will afterwards state the reason why I have mentioned this affair.

Some time afterwards Paul went to Byzantium, and, by the offer of seven centenars of gold, endeavoured to persuade the Emperor to reinstate him in his office, of which he said he had been unjustly deprived. Justinian received the money affably, treated him with respect, and promised to reinstate him as soon as possible, although another at present held the office, as if he did not know that he himself had put to death two of his best friends and supporters, and confiscated their estates. The Emperor exerted all his efforts in this direction, and there did not appear to be the least doubt that Paul would be reinstated. But Vigilius, who at the time was in Byzantium, resolved not to submit to the Emperor's orders in this matter, and declared that it was impossible for him to annul by his own decision a sentence which Pelagius had given in his name. So that, in everything, Justinian's only object was to get money by any means whatsoever.

The following is a similar case. There was a Samaritan by birth, a native of Palestine, who, having been compelled by the law to change his religion, had become a Christian and taken the name of Faustinus. This Faustinus became a member of the senate and governor of Palestine; and when his time of office had expired, on his return to Byzantium he was accused by certain priests of favouring the religion and customs of the Samaritans and of having been guilty of great cruelties towards the Christians in Palestine. Justinian appeared to be very angry and expressed his indignation that, during his reign, anyone should have the audacity to insult the name of Christian. The members of the senate met to examine into the matter, and, at the instance of the Emperor, Faustinus was banished. But Justinian, having received large presents of money from him, immediately annulled the sentence. Faustinus, restored to his former authority and the confidence of the Emperor, was appointed steward of the imperial domains in Palestine and Phoenicia, and was allowed to act in every respect exactly as he pleased. These few instances are sufficient to show how Justinian protected the Christian ordinances.

CHAPTER XXVIII

I must now briefly relate how he unhesitatingly abolished the laws when money was in question. There was in Emesa a man named Priscus, who was an expert forger and very clever in his art. The church of Emesa, many years before, had been instituted sole heir to the property of one of the most distinguished inhabitants named Mammianus, a patrician of noble birth and of great wealth. During the reign of Justinian, Priscus made a list of all the families of the town, taking care to notice which were wealthy and able to disburse large sums. He carefully hunted up the names of their ancestors, and, having found some old documents in their handwriting, forged a number of acknowledgments, in which they confessed that they were largely indebted to Mammianus in sums of money which had been left with them by him as a deposit. The amount of these forged acknowledgments was no less than a hundred centenars of gold. He also imitated in a marvellous manner the handwriting of a public notary, a man of conspicuous honesty and virtue, who during the lifetime of Mammianus used to draw up all their documents for the citizens, sealing them with his own hand, and delivered these forged documents to those who managed the ecclesiastical affairs of Emesa, on condition that he should receive part of the money which might be obtained in this manner.

But, since there was a law which limited all legal processes to a period of thirty years, except in cases of mortgage and certain others, in which the prescription extended to forty years, they resolved to go to Byzantium and, offering a large sum of money to the Emperor, to beg him to assist them in their project of ruining their fellow-citizens.

The Emperor accepted the money, and immediately published a decree which ordained that affairs relating to the Church should not be restricted to the ordinary prescription, but that anything might be recovered, if claimed within a hundred years: which regulation was to be observed not only in Emesa, but throughout the whole of the Roman Empire. In order to see that the new rule was put into execution, he sent Longinus to Emesa, a man of great vigour and bodily strength, who was afterwards made praefect of Byzantium. Those who had the management of the affairs of the church of Emesa, acting upon the forged documents, sued some of the citizens for two centenars of gold, which they were condemned to pay, being unable to raise any objection, by reason of the length of time elapsed and their ignorance of the facts. All the inhabitants, and especially the principal citizens, were in great distress and highly incensed against their accusers. When ruin already threatened the majority of the citizens, Providence came to their assistance in a most unexpected manner. Longinus ordered Priscus, the contriver of this detestable invention, to bring him all the acknowledgments; and, when he showed himself unwilling to do so, he dealt him a violent blow in the face. Priscus, unable to resist the blow dealt by a man of such bodily strength, fell backwards upon the ground, trembling and affrighted. Believing that Longinus had discovered the whole affair, he confessed; and, the whole trick being thus brought to light, the suits were stopped.

Justinian, not content with subverting the laws of the Roman Empire every day, exerted himself in like manner to do away with those of the Jews; for, if Easter came sooner in their calendar than in that of the Christians, he did not allow them to celebrate the Passover on their own proper day or to make their offerings to God, or to perform any of their usual solemnities. The magistrates even inflicted heavy fines upon several of them, upon information that they had eaten the paschal lamb during that time, as if it were an infraction of the laws of the state. Although I could mention countless acts of this nature committed by Justinian, I will not do so, for I must draw my narrative to a close. What I have said will be sufficient to indicate the character of the man.

CHAPTER XXIX

I will, however, mention two instances of his falsehood and hypocrisy.

After having deprived Liberius (of whom I have spoken above) of his office, he put in his place John, an Egyptian by birth, surnamed Laxarion. When Pelagius, who was a particular friend of Liberius, heard of this, he inquired of Justinian whether what he had heard was true. The Emperor immediately denied it, and protested that he had done nothing of the kind. He then gave Pelagius a letter in which Liberius was ordered to hold fast to his government and by no means to give it up, and added that he had no present intention of removing Liberius. At that time there resided in Byzantium an uncle of John named Eudaemon, a man of consular rank and great wealth, who had the management of the imperial estates. Having been informed of what had taken place, he also inquired of the Emperor whether his nephew was assured in his government. Justinian, saying nothing about his letter to Liberius, sent John positive orders to hold fast to his government, since his views were still the same concerning it. Trusting to this, John ordered Liberius to quit the governor's palace, as having been deprived of his office. Liberius refused, placing equal reliance in the Emperor's despatch. John, having armed his followers, marched against Liberius, who defended himself with his guards. An engagement took place, in which several were slain, and amongst them John, the new governor.

At the earnest entreaty of Eudaemon, Liberius was immediately summoned to Byzantium. The matter was investigated before the senate, and Liberius was acquitted, as being only guilty of justifiable homicide in self-defence. Justinian, however, did not let him escape, until he had forced him to give him a considerable sum of money privately. Such was the great respect Justinian showed for the truth, and such was the faithfulness with which he kept his promises. I will here permit myself a brief digression, which may not be irrelevant. This Eudaemon died shortly afterwards, leaving behind him a large number of relatives, but no will, either written or verbal. About the same time, the chief eunuch of the court, named Euphratas, also died intestate; he left behind him a nephew, who would naturally have succeeded to his property, which was considerable. The Emperor took possession of both fortunes, appointing himself sole heir, not even leaving so much as a three-obol piece to the legal inheritors. Such was the respect Justinian showed for the laws and the kinsmen of his intimate friends. In the same manner, without having the least claim to it, he seized the fortune of Irenaeus, who had died some time before.

Another event which took place about this time I cannot omit. There lived at Ascalon a man named Anatolius, the most distinguished member of the senate. His daughter, his only child and heiress, was married to a citizen of Caesarea, named Mamilianus, a man of distinguished family. There was an ancient statute which provided that, whenever a senator died without male issue, the fourth part of his estate should go to the senate of the town, and the rest to the heirs-at-law. On this occasion Justinian gave a striking proof of his character. He had recently made a law which reversed this, that, when a senator died without male issue, the fourth part only should go to the heirs, the three other parts being divided between the senate and the public treasury, although it had never happened before that the estate of any senator had been shared between the public treasury and the Emperor.

Anatolius died while this law was in force. His daughter was preparing to divide her inheritance with the public treasury and the senate of the town in accordance with the law, when she received letters from the senate of Ascalon and from the Emperor himself, in which they resigned all claim to the money, as if they had received their due. Afterwards Mamilianus (the son-in-law of Anatolius) died, leaving one daughter, the legal heiress to his estate. The daughter soon afterwards died, during her mother's lifetime, after having been married to a person of distinction, by whom, however, she had no issue, either male or female. Justinian then immediately seized the whole estate, giving utterance to the strange opinion, that it would be a monstrous thing that the daughter of Anatolius, in her old age, should be enriched by the property of both her husband and father. However, to keep her from want, he ordered that she should receive a stater of gold a day, as long as she lived; and, in the decree whereby he deprived her of all her property, he declared that he bestowed this stater upon her for the sake of religion, seeing that he was always in the habit of acting with piety and virtue.

I will now show that he cared nothing even for the Blue faction, which showed itself devoted to him, when it was a question of money. There was amongst the Cilicians a certain Malthanes, the son-in-law of that Leo who had held the office of "Referendary," whom Justinian commissioned to put down seditious movements in the country. On this pretext, Malthanes treated most of the inhabitants with great cruelty. He robbed them of their wealth, sent part to the Emperor, and claimed the rest for himself. Some endured their grievances in silence; but the inhabitants of Tarsus who belonged to the Blue faction, confident of the protection of the Empress, assembled in the market-place and abused Malthanes, who at the time was not present. When he heard of it, he immediately set out with a body of soldiers, reached Tarsus by night, sent his soldiers into the houses at daybreak, and ordered them to put the inhabitants to death. The Blues, imagining that it was an attack from a foreign foe, defended themselves as best they could. During the dark, amongst other misfortunes, Damianus, a member of the senate and president of the Blues in Tarsus, was slain by an arrow.

When the news reached Byzantium, the Blues assembled in the streets with loud murmurs of indignation, and bitterly complained to the Emperor of the affair, uttering the most violent threats against Leo and Malthanes. The Emperor pretended to be as enraged as they were, and immediately ordered an inquiry to be made into the conduct of the latter. But Leo, by the present of a considerable sum of money, appeased him, so that the process was stopped, and the Emperor ceased to show favour to the Blues. Although the affair remained uninvestigated, the Emperor received Malthanes, who came to Byzantium to pay his respects, with great kindness and treated him with honour. But, as he was leaving the Emperor's presence, the Blues, who had been on the watch, attacked him in the palace, and would certainly have slain him, had not some of their own party, bribed by Leo, prevented them. Who would not consider that state to be in a most pitiable condition, in which the sovereign allows himself to be bribed to leave charges uninvestigated, and in which malcontents venture without hesitation to attack one of the magistrates within the precincts of the palace, and to lay violent hands upon him? However, no punishment was inflicted either upon Malthanes or his assailants, which is a sufficient proof of the character of Justinian.

CHAPTER XXX

His regulations as to the public "posts" and "spies" will show how much he cared for the interests of the state. The earlier Emperors, in order to gain the most speedy information concerning the movements of the enemy in each territory, seditions or unforeseen accidents in individual towns, and the actions of the governors and other officials in all parts of the Empire, and also in order that those who conveyed the yearly tribute might do so without danger or delay, had established a rapid service of public couriers according to the following system: As a day's journey for an active man, they settled eight stages, sometimes fewer, but never less than five. There were forty horses in each stage and a number of grooms in proportion. The couriers who were intrusted with this duty, by making use of relays of excellent horses, frequently covered as much ground in one day by this means as they would otherwise have covered in ten, when carrying out the above commissions. In addition, the landed proprietors in each country, especially those whose estates were in the interior, reaped great benefit from these posts; for, by selling their surplus corn and fruit every year to the state for the support of the horses and grooms, they gained considerable revenue. By this means the state received, without interruption, the tribute due from each, and, in turn, reimbursed those who furnished it, and thus everything was to the advantage of the state. Such was the old system. But Justinian, having commenced by suppressing the post between Chalcedon and Dakibiza, compelled the couriers to carry all despatches from Byzantium to Helenopolis by sea. They unwillingly obeyed; for, being obliged to embark upon small skiffs, such as were generally used for crossing the strait, they ran great risk of being shipwrecked, if they met with stormy weather. For, since great speed was enjoined upon them, they were unable to wait for a favourable opportunity for putting out to sea, when the weather was calm. It is true that he maintained the primitive system on the road to Persia, but for the rest of the East, as far as Egypt, he reduced the number of posts to one, for a day's journey, and substituted a few asses for the horses, so that the report of what was taking place in each district only reached Byzantium with difficulty and long after the events had occurred, when it was too late to apply any remedy; and, on the other hand, the owners of estates found no benefit from their products, which were either spoilt or lay idle.

The spies were organized in the following manner: A number of men used to be supported at the state's expense, whose business it was to visit hostile countries, especially the court of Persia, on pretence of business or some other excuse, and to observe accurately what was going on; and by this means, on their return, they were able to report to the Emperors all the secret plans of their enemies, and the former, being warned in advance, took precautions and were never surprised. This system had long been in vogue amongst the Medes. Chosroes, by giving larger salaries to his spies, none of whom were born Romans, reaped great benefit from this precaution. Justinian, having discontinued this practice, lost considerable territory, especially the country of the Lazes, which was taken by the enemy, since the Romans had no information where the King and his army were. The state also formerly kept a large number of camels, which carried the baggage on the occasion of an expedition into an hostile country. By this means the peasants were relieved from the necessity of carrying burdens, and the soldiers were well supplied with necessaries. Justinian, however, did away with nearly all the camels, so that, when the army is marching against an enemy, everything is in an unsatisfactory condition. Such was the care he took of the most important state institutions. It will not be out of place to mention one of his ridiculous acts. There was at Caesarea a lawyer named

Evangelius, a person of distinction, who, by the favour of fortune, had amassed great riches and considerable landed estates. He afterwards purchased, for three centenars of gold, a village on the coast named Porphyreon. When Justinian heard of this, he immediately took it from him, only returning him a small portion of the price he had paid for it, at the same time declaring that it was unseemly that such a village should belong to Evangelius the lawyer. But enough of this. It remains to speak of certain innovations introduced by Justinian and Theodora. Formerly, when the senate had audience of the Emperor, it paid him homage in the following manner: Every patrician kissed him on the right breast, and the Emperor, having kissed him on the head, dismissed him; all the rest bent the right knee before the Emperor and retired. As for the Empress, it was not customary to do homage to her. But those who were admitted to the presence of this royal pair, even those of patrician rank, were obliged to prostrate themselves upon their face, with hands and feet stretched out; and, after having kissed both his feet, they rose up and withdrew. Nor did Theodora refuse this honour. She received the ambassadors of the Persians and other barbarian nations and (a thing which had never been done before) bestowed magnificent presents upon them, as if she had been absolute mistress of the Empire. Formerly, those who associated with the Emperor called him Imperator and the Empress Imperatrix, and the other officials according to their rank. But if anyone addressed either Justinian or Theodora without the addition of the title Sovereign Lord or Sovereign Lady, or without calling himself their slave, he was looked upon as ignorant and insolent in his language, and, as if he had committed a very grave offence and insulted those whom it least became him, he was dismissed. Formerly, only a few were granted admission to the palace, and that with difficulty; but, from the time of the accession of Justinian and Theodora, the magistrates and all other persons were continually in the palace. The reason was, that formerly the magistrates freely administered justice and laws independently, and executed the customary sentences at their own residences, and the subjects, seeing and hearing that no injustice would be done to them, had little reason to trouble the Emperor. But this pair, taking control of all business to themselves in order that they might ruin their subjects, forced them to humiliate themselves before them in a most servile manner. Thus the courts of justice were empty nearly every day, and hardly a person was to be seen in them, while in the palace there were crowds of men pushing and abusing one another, all endeavouring to be foremost in showing their servility. Those who were on the most intimate terms with the Imperial pair remained the whole day and a great part of the night, without food or sleep, until they were worn out, and this apparent good fortune was their only reward. Others, who were free from all these cares and anxieties, were puzzled to think what had become of the wealth and treasures of the Empire. Some declared that it had all fallen into the hands of the barbarians, while others asserted that the Emperor kept it locked up in secret hiding-places of his own. When Justinian, whether he be man or devil, shall have departed this life, those who are then living will be able to learn the truth.

NOTES

[1: By Mr. Hodgkin, "Italy and her Invaders," vol. iii., p. 638.]

[2: The best modern authorities are agreed that he was really the author.]

[3: Or, rather, three, the fourth being only a kind of supplement.]

[4: As internal evidence in favour of the identity of the author of the "Secret History," and the "Wars" and "Buildings," the few following points, amongst many, may be noticed. The reference in the preface to the "History of the Wars," that the author was born at Caesarea, is more closely defined by the statement in the "Secret History" that he was from Caesarea in Palestine; in both works an account of the relations of Justinian to the Church is promised, but the promise is not fulfilled. The "Secret History" refers to the extravagant "building" mania of the Emperor. In all three works we meet with a constant recurrence of the same ideas, the same outspoken language, greatly embittered in the "Secret History," the same fanatical pragmatism, the same association of luck, destiny, and divinity, of guilt and expiation, the same superstition in the forms of demonology, belief in dreams and miracles, and lastly the same commonplaces, expressions, and isolated words.]

[5: "Decline and Fall," chap. xl.]

[6: The Ædificia, or "Buildings," of Justinian.]

[7: The article on Procopius in the "Encyclopaedia Britannica" (9th edition) by Professor Bryce should also be consulted.]

[8: Spearmen, lancers.]

[9: Shield-bearers.]

[10: Or "Count," Master of the royal stables.]

[11: Pumpkin.]

[12: Private secretaries.]

[13: Syn[=o]n[=e].]

[14: Epibol[=e].]

[15: Diagraph[=e].]

[16: Here the text is corrupt.]

[17: Chancellors, or, Commissioners.]

[18: Shears, scissors.]